PROBLEMS OF RURAL AGED

PROBLEMS OF RURAL AGED
A Sociological Perspective

VENKATESWARLU VANKAYALAPATI

KALPAZ PUBLICATIONS
DELHI-110052

Problems of Rural Aged

ISBN: 81-7835-677-5

Published in 2008 in India by
Kalpaz Publications
C-30, Satyawati Nagar,
Delhi-110052
E-mail: kalpaz@hotmail.com
Phone : 9212729499

Lasser Type Setting by: Rudra Computer Graphics, Delhi
Printed at : Singhal Print Media, Delhi

Dedicated to my Mother

Late Smt. Venkata Ratnam Vankayalapati

Contents

Foreword
Preface
Prologue

1 **Understanding Gerontology**
• Definitional Problems-old Age • Concept of Gerontology • Multi-disciplinary Nature of Ageing • What is Age, Old age and Ageing? • History of Gerontology and Geriatrics • The Global Context • Background • Development of Age • Sociology of Ageing in India: Perspective and Policy Options • The Sociological Turn • A Social Process • Sociological Perspectives on Ageing • Definitional Problems and Conceptualisations • The Myth of the Aging Mind

2 **Plight of Old Aged in India**
• Traditional Approach • Indebtedness • The National Situation • Improving Support Systems in India • Ageing in India: Some Reflections • Existing Programmes on Ageing • Constitutuional Provisions • Legislative Measures • Policy measure • Reading Future Options • Indian Elderly and Various Role Situations • Roles Overload • Role Isolation • Role expectation • Role Conflict • Population Aging

3 **Social and Health Perspectives of Elderly**
• Ageing Some Socio Economic Issues • The Old and Physical – Social Changes • Ageing Modernization and Role Play • A Socially Determined Category • Social Networks and the Aged in India • Role of Elderly • The Health Myth • Lack of Medical Aid and Poor Diet • Health Services: Availability and Access - AGED • Nutrition and Ageing - AGED • Optimal Diet • Myths about Aged Persons • Social Myths

4 **Coping with Old Age**
• Healthy Ageing • Elderly and Community Mental Health • Criteria of Adjustment • The Future of Ageing • Use of Indigenous and Innovative Ideas • Self - Reliance – What Seniors can do for Themselves • Developing Inner Strength • In Search of Better Living for the Aged • Apprehension about Becoming Old • Markers of Old Age • Strategy • Successful Ageing

5 **Senior Citizens**
• Role of Family • Neighbourhood and Society • Government's Duty Towards Senior Citizens • Senior Citizens Helping Themselves • Senior Citizens • Objectives for Mobilization • Assessment of Resources • Man Power • Finance • Government Initiatives • Other Agencies • Utiliazation of Resources • Mechanics of Mobilization • Terms of Reference • Motivation • The Aged and Society

6 **Collective Approach of Senior Citizens**
• Comprehensive Approach • Need for Data on the Elderly • Globalisation and the Aged • Globalisation – its Meaning • Globalization – Its Impact on Aged

• Development of the Aged People – Strategies and Approaches • Employment Opportunities for Senior Citizens Pose Problems on Following Accounts

7 **Enervated Approach of Senior Citizens**
• The Economic Myth • The Health Myth • Mobilizing Senior Citizens for their Own Cause • Family System • Social Involvement

8 **Policies and Programmes for the Aged in India**
• The National Policy on Older Persons • Emerging Problem of Care of the Aging • Constitutional and Legislative Provisions • Plan Policy • Approach and Strategy • Laws Relating to Elderly • Attitude Towards the Aged Youth Attitudes and perception towards Elderly

9 **Lonely Elders**
• Aging—Weaker Sections • Who were those that Supported the old? • Living Arrangements • Conceptualisation of Aging

10 **Life as Retiree**
• Problems of Retired Men • Views and Comments of Retired Men • Learning from the Experience • Housing and Environments

11 **Urban Rural Disparity**
• The Urban Scene• Deprived of the Deprived Rural Aged • Housing for the Aging • Specific Needs • Measures to Mitigate Housing Problems of the Aging • Special Housing Schemes for the Aging • Special Planning and Design Considerations • Research and Development Work

12 **Problems of Widows-Child less Widows**
• Widowhood (Vaidhavya)

13 **The Voluntary Organizations and Older Persons**
• Bharat Pensioners' Samaj • Caritas India • The Indian Association of Retired Persons • Age-care • The AgeWell Foundation • Help age India • Formatin of a Typical Senior Citizens Organizations • Sphere of Activities of Senior Citizens' Organizations • Routine Activities • Socially Oriented Programmes • Special Programs on Occasions • Apex Bodies of Senior Citizens' Organizations • How can the Government Help Mobilization • Towards Active Ageing • Social Welfare

Index

Foreword

It gives me immense pleasure that this volume authored by Dr. V. Venkateswarlu, Teaching Associate, Department of Sociology, Acharya Nagarjuna University is brought out by the publishers at the appropriate time when the aging population is increasing at alarming rates attracting the attention of social scientists, demographers and policy makers. The increasing numbers and proportions of Aging caused by improved living conditions and advancement of medical science produce not only beneficial effects but also pose serious problems to the aging population particularly to the disadvantaged and deprived sections in terms of their adjustment to the family and the society, deterioration of health, economic and social support, the quality of life, life satisfaction, psychic isolation, feelings of alienation and deprivation in myriad forms. The author has highlighted these problems by his empirical research in the rural population of Andhra Pradesh. The author points out that the challenge of Aging for developing countries is of greater concern when compared to developed countries since the poverty groups particularly the deprived of the deprived aged such as widowed, divorced, separated and never married are the worst sufferers facing all sorts of humiliations and hardships due to lack of familial and social support.

The researcher has rightly brought out the gender differences by making comparative analysis of the problems of Aging by pointing out the relative deprivation of the aged females in respect of their access to necessities of life, social participation, medical care and sharing of resources of the family. Besides, the empirical research and analysis of statistical data, the author appropriately added case studies supplementing the macro level analysis by bringing forth and focussing on the life situations of the problems and difficulties confronting the aged in rural scenario.

The present volume explores the knowledge about the problems, perspectives and the life situations of the rural aged. I appreciate the strenuous efforts made by the author in bringing out this volume at a time when we need to show serious concern for this global phenomena of growing problems of greying population.

I hope that this volume would serve the needs of all agencies, people including teachers, students, social scientists, social workers, social activists and policy makers working for the cause of the aging population for taking appropriate action for ameliorating the suffering and hardship they face.

Prof. V. BALAMOHANDAS
Vice-Chancellor
Acharya Nagarjuna University

Preface

The ageing of a population is an inevitable consequence of process of demographic transition and creates an imbalance in the age structure over a period if time. India is a country with fine tradition of respecting, loving and supporting the aged. The joint or extended families of several generations under the same roof was basic unit of production and livelihood in traditional agricultural society in ancient India. In recent times, as a result of changing circumstances due to demographic transition, rapid pace of industrialization and urbanization, disintegration of joint or extended family structures into nuclear ones, the older people have become increasingly vulnerable not only to the physical disabilities but also to social, economic and emotional alienation and isolation. Given this concern this book attempts to present a comprehensive account of the elderly Life in India.

Behind every research there are number of professors, collegues, friends and respondents, who provide invaluable support and assistance.

At the outset, I express my deep sense of gratitude to Prof. M. Lakshmipathi Raju, Head, Department of sociology, social work and I.R.P.M, Acharya Nagarjuna University for his constant guidance and supervision at every stage of this research work and having with in prologue to this book. Hence the author is in deep intellectual debt to Prof. M. Lakshmipathi Raju without whose guidance this book would have not materialized.

It is my profound privilege to express heartfelt gratitude to Prof. M. Indira Devi, Retired Professor, dept. of sociology, Andhra University, for her unstinted support, succor and constant guidance in completion of this book.

It gives me a great pleasure to express my heartfelt respects and deep gratitude to Prof. V. Balamohan Das, Vice chancellor, Acharya Nagarjuna University, Guntur for his graciously consenting to write a foreword for this book and thereby adding significant contribution to this volume.

I express my sincere thanks to Professors of Acharya Nagarjuna University Prof. Y.R. Hara Gopal Reddy Rector, Acharya Nagarjuna University, Prof. M.K Durga Prasad Principal, Acharya Nagarjuna University college, Prof. N. Samuyelu, Executivecouncil Member, Prof. M. Koteswara Rao, Department of Adult Education, A.N.U. for their encouragement in completion of the book.

I acknowledge my heartful thanks to Prof. P.V Ramamurthy, Prof. Troisi, Prof. T.S. Nair, Prof. Gary Andrews, Dr. S.D. Gokhale, Dr. D. Jamuna, resource persons in the training programme conducted by Sri Venkateswara University, giving their valuable suggestions on the Gerontological concepts used in the present study.

My special thanks are particularly due to Dr P. Narasimha Rao, Department of Economics, Acharya Nagarjuna University for his unstinct co-operation and encouragement throughout my research work.

Last but not least I should not forget the sacrifices made by all my family members particularly my wife Prasuna, daughter Sravani, parents, Brothers sisters-in-law, brother-in law and sister for the discomfort caused to them in materializing this book. I thank them for bearing with the inconvenience and encouraged me during my publication of this book.

V. Venkateswarlu

Prologue

I have gone through the whole script of the book authored by my collegue Dr. V. Venkateswarlu with keen interest and attention since I was actively involved in guiding the research project at every stage and this volume is the outcome of his research work. I have found the author putting his heart and soul in preparation of the volume by his strenuous efforts for gathering the extensive literature on the subjcct and also taking meticulous care in collection of data in the field facing several hardships in visiting the remote villages for meeting and interviewing the respondents. He has adopted rigorous methodology for the study in formulating the research and sampling design and the application of appropriate of statistical techniques in the analysis of data.

The author highlights the problems of the rural aged in various dimensions, categorically dealing with the gender discrimination, access to the family and community resources, estrangement in familial and social relationships, psychic isolation, feelings of alienation, deprivation of economic and social supports, deterioration of health, proneness to physical ailments caused by the advancement of age .With advanced years of age the social participation and sphere of their social activities become restricted since their importance in the family and society decreases in all respects In terms of their role,

Employment earning capacity, possession of assets, sharing of resources and responsibilities and hence they are labeled as unwanted, burdensome and playing "Role less role".

The author has rightly pointed out the miserable conditions and plight of the aged persons belonging to low-income families and poverty groups who face hardships and degradation of life since they are not only deprived of means of livelihood but also alienated from family support. As evidenced by the case studies, some of them were found resorting to begging and depending on relatives and friends. The widowed, divorced, separated, the never married and persons living alone are the worst sufferers and they may be termed as deprived of the deprived aged.

The author spells out various rehabilitative and welfare measures for ameliorating the conditions of the aged in the unorganized sector by strengthening the family; social and economic supports and involving them in developmental activities.

I congratulate the author for the way in which he has carried out his empirical study and brought out this present volume which would serve the interests of all those particularly teachers, students, researchers, social scientists, social workers, social activists, demographers, who are working for the cause of the senior citizens.

M. Lakshmipathi Raju

1

Understanding Gerontology

Definitional Problems-old Age

When is a person old? When does one et categorized as elderly? What does category / concept of aged refer to ? Can it be used as a coherent category? This section looks at some of these questions.

From time to time, scholars have employed different definitions of aged', 'elderly,' 'old,' and no one can claim to have a patent over the definition. The variety of definitions offered in gerontological literature is almost as diverse as the number of writers. Thus, adding confusion to an already difficult nomenclature. "Adults delude that old age can be put off until an indeterminate moment, and for young people, this does not exist at all on their horizon" (Elorea, 1980:234). Simply stated, 'aged' means the state of being elderly, in scientific terms, its use is a non sequitur. Whether a person is perceived to be elderly or not depends upon the observer's eye. There exists no clear-cut demarcation of age upon the attainment of which a person can be called 'old,' 'elderly,' or 'aged'. Nor is there a biologically determined age limit that classifies a person as elderly.

The definition of the term 'elderly' or 'aged' varies from society to society. Ancient Chinese scholars delineated seven phases in a man's life, and Pythagoras in the sixth century B.C. compared human life to the seasons. In both cases, old age was deemed to be beyond 60 years (Stub, 1982). Some societies still treat 40 or 50 years as marking the transition into old age. "In Thai society, old age begins at 60 years. Age is computed in 12-year (animal year cycles), with the 60th birthday making the completion of the fifth cycle and beginning of the sixth (Chayovan, Knodel and Siriboon, 1990:3). After reaching this age, a person is addressed by younger persons with special terms of respect, the equivalent of the kinship terms grandfather or grandmother, even though the speaker may' not be related to the older person in any way of kinship" (Wongsith and Saengtienchai, 1994:430).

Indonesia uses 60 years as a cut-off point to classify people as old. Being a country where the majority of people are Moslems, the age of the Prophet Muhammad is often used as a reference. The prophet is said to have passed away at the age of 63 (Wirosuhardia, 1994:88). In western industrialized nations, the typical onset of old age is reckoned at 65 years.

Guha Roy (1991) observes, "The definition of old age is very much dependent on its use in a particular context. Way of fixing the entry into old age based on retirement, however, ignores the large number of women have not been in the gainful occupation and that the age of retirement varies not only between countries but also between public and private sectors within a country".

A survey of some studies conducted by some scholars in India also highlights the fact that it is really difficult to draw a dividing line uniformly to categorise the 'elderly.' The range of variation extends from 39 years to 51 years at the lower end. For Marulasiddaiah (1968) it is 55 years and above; for Jatana et a1. (1991) it is 51 years; Prakash (1987, 1991) puts it as 50 years for Women and 60 for men; Sen (1991) uses 39 years as the dividing line; for Easwaramoorthy (1991) it varies between 58 and 70 years Barai (1991) and Patil et a1. (1991) treat 60 years as the age limit for an individual to be treated as 'elderly' or 'old'. The census (of India) uses 60 years as a cut-off point to classify people as old. For purposes of being eligible for old age pension (OAP) most of the states in India have laid down 65 years as the minimum age, while in a few states the age limit is fixed at 60 years (Arora, 1993). Scholars such as Gokhale (1994:78) point out, the "for statistical analysis 60 is a convenient age. But old age is a very relative concept. The process of continuing physiological, psychological and social change throughout the life-span with great variations, occurs among individuals."

What is considered old age varies between countries because of different social, economic, and historical situations and conditions. Each society divides the life span into a definite number of stages embedded in the culture. It assigns a meaning to these stages and defines, for individuals, the conditions of transition from one stage to another during the life course, that is, the socially organized life-span. Old age designates the last stage and thus has to be understood as a continually renegotiated social construction.

Old age itself, has become clearly distinguished as a specific stage of life, and delimited chronologically, with the result of a sharp tripartite division of the life cycle into a phase of preparation, followed by the one of productive activity in economic/income generating terms, and finally, the stage of retirement. In many countries the definition of elderly persons is closely related to their position in the labour market; thus persons on their retirement are regarded as elderly. Official definitions of the elderly refer to people of post-productive age that is of retirement age. The collective definition of the elderly is based on three criteria: retired from work and drawing a pension, looking old and having some limitation in activities of daily living.

The chronological criterion for classifying an individual or a collectively as 'aged' or "elderly' is the operational means generally employed for administrative purposes - pensions, insurance, and the like. For administrative purposes each country tends to fix an age limit for working life of a person to suit its own interests. Here the phrase 'old age' is socially defined by the transition from salaried work to retirement. This definition masks the fact that a large number of men and women who have been or are generally outside the ambit of gainful employment, and do not retire at a formal age. This also applies to those engaged in the unorganized sector. It is interesting to note that the age of retirement even in the formal sector shows considerable variation.

This categorization is difficult to apply in the Indian context, firstly, because the majority of the elderly, especially elderly women have not gone to school and often do not know their chronological age. Second, the concept applies mainly to people employed in the formal sector in India, very few elderly people-more so elderly women—are employed in the formal sector. For the majority of a population whose activities are confined to the urban informal sector or to the rural agricultural sector, work activity continues until extremely advanced ages when they are disabled and can no longer work. It is, therefore, necessary to develop realistic and meaningful measures that accurately describe the elderly in India. The categorization of the ageing population should reflect the local communities' perception of the ageing process.

The 'old' or 'aged' is a relative term and generally used in relation to young. It is really difficult to draw a dividing line uniformly for all communities. Available research shows that people grow old at different rates. One person may be physically old at 60 while another is 'young' at 70. "It is really difficult to define old age. It is not exclusively biological, nor is it controlled by the calendar. One's enviroments can make one old; old age is not just the heritage of others but of ourselves" (Jain,1986:B-2). It is true that no part of the human organism can escape from the decline caused by ageing, yet the ageing process is 'disorganised' in the sense that one part of the human organism may decline at different times and rates. It is impossible to set any meaningful age designation, either for the beginning of degenerative changes associated with increasing age.

Biological, psychological and sociological processes continue to distinguish individuals at any chronological point in their life. There are no definite biological or psychological or socio-cultural parameters which individually or collectively can demarcate the particular chronological age uniformly. Being a relative criterion, the concept of aged will differ from species to species, as the life expectancy, longevity and life-span also differ. The concept of aged in man varies with purpose and view point and also sex, residence, climate and the life. It varies between urban and rural people (Biswas, 1987). Even it is conceived differently by the old and non-old (mature/adult young).

The classification of a person or a group of persons as elderly by reasons of age and the extent of ability is determined by such factors as level of socio-economic development, living conditions, nutrition, health services, cultural factors and the nature of work.

In non-literate societies there is hardly any conceptualization of absolute age calculated by time elapsed from a fixed position such as date of birth. Members of primitive tribes often do not know how old they are. Old age is, generally determined by physical and mental conditions rather than chronological age. Indeed the idea of keeping a precise account of age is a relatively recent one.

In rural India, people are not classified as 'aged' by an absolute biological or chronological criterion—as most do not know how old they are. They are, however, generally aware of their relative age and the category and activities appropriate to their contemporaries and the progress made through the life-cycle of their kin in the adjacent generations. Age is sometimes reckoned by an association of a person's birth with special historic events, or geo-climatic, astronomical occurance, eclipses, full-moon floods, earthquakes, droughts, or with socio-cultural events—festivals, rituals and the like. It is the changing status of these people—parents and children that defines an individual as an elder; here, the status is a relational one.

The cultural markers for distinguishing an 'elderly' or 'aged' vary from society to society, as they are dependent on one life expectancy as well as longevity of population in different societies. For example, in a society with a life expectancy of 70 years, the 'older person' is likely to be much younger in a society with a life expectancy of 70 years. Old age is often determined by cultural norms prevailing in a society. Differences among people in different cultural groups within any society do not suddenly emerge in old age, but reflect cumulative lifetime experiences. In Indian society, marriage of one's children, particularly the eldest son's and bringing in of the daughter-in-law, marks the beginning of old age for women far more clearly than does a specified number of years. Accordingly, role expectations change for male and female members in a household.

Among a few communities of South India, especially the Brahmans of Karnataka and Tamilnadu, a ceremony called Shashtya-badi Purthi is observed to celebrate the 60th birthday because it is customarily treated as second birth of an individual.

The term 'aged' not only describes individuals but also is used as a collective noun, and once individuals are identified as 'old' they are perceived exclusively as such. Hazan (1994: 16) observes there are several ways of defining aged. "One way is the seemingly unproblematic self definition: an "old person" is someone who regards him-or herself as such... Another definition of 'aged' is socially constructed, composed of an infinite number of overlapping points of view with regard to a given person. Changing circumstances and the dynamics of social relationships make it difficult if not impossible to use such a definition rigorously."

Usage of the terms 'old,' 'senior citizens,' 'aged,' elderly,' "retired', 'geriatric,' 'pensioner,' is common both in popular and academic discourses. The general impression conveyed by the terms 'elderly' or 'aged' is one of homogeneity, whereas in actuality it is characterized by diversity. The period of old age covers a long span of life. The 'aged' is a varied body. Heterogeneity abounds among the elderly, not only along the life cycle but also in space as well. The aged may have features linked to a generation, gender, and social environment. They are a large and heterogeneous population with varying types of needs ranging from health promotion and maintenance to long-term care for irreversible dementias and other incapacities. A wide array of cultural, linguistic, occupational, educational, regional diversities as also gender variations are often noticed within the elderly population. Singly as well as collectively these factors, affect the individual, and have a considerable bearing on the life process of the individual. Their impact can be favourable at times and in given situations, while it can be adverse at times.

Further, the aged are not a cohesive group. They may be composed of several generations, each of them having its own history, different standards of living throughout the life-course and different values giving rise to different behaviours. The life circumstances of the elderly vary considerably. We cannot expect uniformity across the generations or even individuals in what are taken to be central or peripheral attributes of elderliness. Euphemisms such as the 'elderly' and senior citizens,' 'aged,' 'old,' are inadequate to describe the multitude of qualities found in aged individuals. One has to be sensitive to variations in age (however defined), circumstances, experiences and indeed age identifications within the groups one terms 'old,' 'aged' or 'elderly'.

In developed countries the elderly persons are divided into three or more categories, viz., the 'young-old', the 'middle-old,' the 'old-old' and the 'very old'. The 'young-old' category comprises of persons in the age group 60-69, who maintain working capability after their retirement. As of 1990, India had 38-39 million in this category. The 'middle-old' consists of persons aged between 70 and 75. The 'old-old' category comprises of individuals aged over 75, who are likely to he frail, and possibly be a victim of physical disabilities and mental illness associated with old age. And finally, the 'very-old' category constituted by individuals who arc 80 years and above.

Most developed countries to define the beginning of old age often use the calendar age of 65. However, some developed countries use different ages, some less than 65, some more. Shanas (1980: 10) observes, "The use of age 65 rather than another age, for instance, 70 as the mark of old age, then, is a man-made artefact." The choice of the calendar age sixty-five to symbolize the beginning of old age is a cultural definition. There is no evidence that the onset of old age is related to any particular year in the life span.

On the other hand, developing countries commonly recognize that a person attaining the age of 60 has become old. This age is also characterized by the time from which the capacity to do work begins to decline. The measure of age in modern societies is chronological age rather than a person's capabilities. The disadvantage of using chronological age as a guide, however, is that the problems associated with all people at some predetermined age (De Loach et al., 1983). Scholars in the field have posited the need for a definition of old age based on function rather than one based on the calendar. However, what the components of such a definition should be are as yet to be determined (Birren and Renner, 1977).

In attempting to decide who is elderly it is important to focus upon functional capability rather than chronological age. For the purpose of this discussion, at least two factors can be mentioned: One, the elderly constitute that age group for which disability is most common. Old age is often viewed as a gradual loss of physical and mental abilities with an increasing difficulty to maintain mobility and independence. WHO (1967) defined old age as, "The period of life when impairment of mental and physical function becomes increasingly manifest by comparison with previous periods of life." It is considered an assortment of diseases and disabilities leading to dependency in later life. The majority of disorders occurring in the elderly people are not solely due to ageing process which would minimize the pathogenicity and incidence of the ailments (Fried and Bush, 1988).

The incidence of disability increases as people get older. Second, "older people face the same social stigma, prejudice, and stereotyping that people who are disabled encounter" (Benedict and Gankos, 1981). The older persons, effective performance in various life-roles, by these negative reactions and attitudes from society can greatly be hindered and thus act as real handicaps (De Loach et al., 1983). De Loach el al., (1983:9) point out that, "This combination of functional and social problem encountered by older people leads to a definition of elderly emphasizing functional issues... The term "elderly" refers to that point in life when the functional limitations that tend to be associated with advanced age present a significant handicap to the individual in relation to his or her desired roles in life."

Because of the variation in ageing from the biological viewpoint it does not make much sense to attempt to state in terms of years just when old age begins. The arbitrary selection of a given age, say sixty or seventy, means that for some individuals old age lasts but few years, whereas, for others it may be thirty or more years in length. (Cavan et al., 1949). Accordingly, physical old age must be considered as only one of several criteria of old age. Wassan (1969) underscores the fact that it is the occupation one is engaged in or the socio-occupational activities pursued that will determine oldness.

Concept of Gerontology

The term gerontology is derived from the Greek word "geras" meaning "old age" and 'logos' referring to the study of the subject. The term gerontology is very broad and encompasses the psychological, socio-economic and physiological aspects of old age. Social gerontology is concerned with reciprocal relationship between the individual and society. The term Geriatrics deals with causes and remedies of physical pathology in old age. Senescence a biological term refers to the physiological aspect of growing old; Gerontocracy refers to Government that is ruled by elders. Ageing is discrimination against individual on basis of old age. The term gerontophobia is used to designate the fear of growing old or fear of hatred of the aged. The term ageing refers to the process of growing old (James, E, Birren, K, Warner Schaie, 1996, 6-10).

Multi-disciplinary Nature of Ageing

The study of ageing is multi-disciplinary, composed of three kinds of ageing: biological, psychological and social, (Int. Enc. Of the Soc. Sci. 1968: 177). As the number of elderly people in Europe and North America grew large enough to justify another branch of medicine, a "new specially, called gerontology from the Greek geron (an old man) became a respected science" (Milne and Milne, 1968: 213), Tibbits (1960) sees Psychological age in terms of the individuals adaptive capacities and social age in terms of social habits and roles.

"The idea that individuals develop and age with variations around an average trend was a powerful conceptual innovation of the early nineteenth century". (Int. Enc. of the Soc. Sci. 1968: 177) but with the increasingly global and mobile population, the validity of the perceived "average trend" may be called into question as may be the notion of "normal life cycle of events", with the adults moving forward in time, successively making educational and occupational choices, marrying, having children and advancing in occupation and then retiring (Int. Enc. of the Soc. Sci. 1968: 178-179). Even the name gerontology has as reference point "an old man". And the linear progression through the life cycle stages fits the "traditional male" better than it would the "traditional female". There are cultural differences in the degree to which legal restrictions and social pressures limit certain social groups-career choices even to day. How then should we look at age and ageing?

What is Age, Old age and Ageing?

How can we study an area in which the subject matter is so poorly defined? While "age" one of the basic demographic facts, it is also one of the "most complicated and complicating of data" (Hardy, 1997: 98). "The state of current research consists of a large number of studies and perspectives" (Kenyon, 1988. 3). Viewing the theoretical developments in Psychology, Schroots, (1996:742) states that "there are three foci-the aged, the age, and ageing" each with their own conceptual problems. Ageing is an integral part of human condition, because of its phenomenological nature and theorists have overlooked the need to define "old", "older" "elderly". Even grammatically, it is incorrect to speak of "older people" without defining "older then whom", yet it is done all the time. Although there is no universally accepted threshhold at which people are labeled "old", societal age norms do in fact exist.

History of Gerontology and Geriatrics

Ignatz A Nascher, the father of modern geriatric medical research and practice, coined the word 'Geriatrics' in 1909 and gave a new name in the medical field, the field was still called ageing and apparently unnoticed until N.A. Rynikow the originator of the term outlined the nature of this new discipline. Gerontology aims at the investigation of the conditioning causes of old age as well as the study and careful description of the regular progress of the changes in behaviour peculiar to age. Despite the fact the research and publication of studies on various aspects of ageing grew rapidly in the late 1920s and 1930s, the discipline of gerontology was not formally recognized nor was the name used in any form until 1940. In 1945, the gerontological society was organized and in 1946, the journal of Gerontlogy made its first appearance (Sati, P.N> 1988).

Edward J. Stieglitz in his work on 'Geriatric Medicine' (1954) used the expression of social gerontology. He divided gerontology in to three major areas, namely, (i) Geriatric medicine, (ii) Biology of senescence, and (iii) Social gerontology. All economic and cultural factors of ageing such as employment, retirement, chronic illness, housing, and education for senescence, marriage, family attitudes towards the aged, social attitudes, cultural maturation and international aspects of maturing population comprise social gerontology. (ati, P.N., 1988). The growing interest and attention of social scientists in 1940s and 1950s to gerontology led to the creation of an Inter-University Training Institute in Social Gerontology in 1957 (Frank L.L., 1946). The publication in 1948 of Social Science Research Council's Planning Report, Social Adjustment in old age edited by Otto Pollak marked another transition from concern about the aged to the study of ageing as a process. At the end of 1950s, a multi-university consortium projected three volumes documenting the scope, methods and conceptualization of studies on ageing. These volumes constitute an excellent bibliographic coverage of studies on ageing prior to their publication and document the principal characteristics of studies of ageing. (Sati, P.N. 1988). Duke and Chicago concentrated on adaptation in late life, conceptualized on morale, mental health or life satisfaction. The dominant perspective, which emerged in these studies, was that social integration in late life is not only possible but also probable and that social integration predicts morale. The exception to this perspective was of course cumming and Henry's (1961) concept of disengagement. Irving Rosow's Social Integration of Aged, states that the probability of social interaction of older persons is significantly affected by the availability of age peers as similar social status. (Sati, P.N. 1988).

The Global Context

The over 100 years aged population of Japan was 153 in 1963. In 1996 this became 7,400. At this point the average population ratio of above 65 years population and the rest was 1:6 it is expected to become 1:4 in 12 years. In Britain, the compulsory retirement age for men was 65 years and for women was 60 years. Of those above 65 years, 95% stayed in dwellings rather than in hospital or homes for the elderly. Less than 7% of those aged more than 80 years show profound symptoms of senile degeneration. Workers who were more than 60 years of age had better working ability than other workers and their attendance was better. In USA, the total number of those aged more than 65 years was 35 million, and it is expected to double by 2030 A.D. Of these, people aged more than 85 years was 4 million in number. This is also expected to double y 2030 A.D. (Srivastava, 2000:22).

A study by Van Willigen (2000: 28) in USA shows that 40% of the aged live alone or with non-relatives. It was proposed that jointness of family requires wealth and a patriarchial social structure. It was also found that 5% of those aged more than 65 years live in nursing homes or old age homes. Three-fourths are more than 75 years old. 34% of them are 85 years and older women.

The U.N. estimates and projections show that in 1995, children were 31.3% of the world's population. The elderly were 9.5% of the world's population. In 2050, children would be 20.5% of the total while the elderly would be 20.7% of the total. In 2100, there would be 18.3% children and 27.7% elderly in the total population. By 2150, there would be 17.5% children and 30.5% elderly in the total population (Bose, 2000).

Groups of countries were created by the U.N. in Group I, Europe, North America and oceania were included. According to the projection in Group I countries 18.8% people were below 25 years, while 18.9% were above 60 years of age. In Group II, Africa, Latin America, China, India, Asia (except Japan) were included. By 2000 A.D., the young were 32.9% while aged are 8%. By 2075 A.D., the young are going to be 19.1% while the aged will be 24.2% of the total (Bose, 2000).

In some developed countries more than 15% of the total population is over 65 years old. 3.4% of the populations are over 80 years. The percentage of the elderly in developing countries is substantially lower than in developing countries. By 1988 there was an estimated 159 million people of over 65 years of age in developing countries and over 60% of the monthly global net increase in older persons was in the developing countries. Between 1990 and 2025 A.D., the percentage of population aged more than 65 years was expected to increase to just over 20% in Europe and North America and to double from 5 to 10% in Asia, Latin America and the Caribbean. By 2020 A.D. there would be 470 million people aged 65 years and more in developing countries, more than double that of developed countries. 3 of the 4 countries projected to have the largest number of old people in the year are China, India and Indonesia (Joshi and Sengupta, 2000).

In most developing countries, more than 50% of the women aged 65 years or more are widowed and in some countries more than 75% of the women aged 75 years or more are widowed. There is no country in which more than 40% of men who are 75 years or more are single. "In most developed countries, there are about 65 men for every 100 women in the age group of 65 and above" (Joshi and Sengupta; 2000:41).

In developing countries the proportion o0f persons aged more than 65 years of age who live alone range from 10% in Japan to 90% in Sweden. It is smaller in developing countries with a tradition of multigenerational households and both married and widowed older persons commonly live with their children and grandchildren. The life expectancy at birth in most developed countries is 70-75 years for men and 76-81 years for women. It is 11 years less in developing countries (Joshi and Sengupta, 2000).

France took 115 years to double its older person's population from 7% to 14%. China, Thailand and Colombia took 25 years (Nampudakani, 1999).

The average life expectancy at birth in 1950 was 46.5 years. This is expected to be 66.5 years in 2000 and 73 years in 2020 A.D. By 2000 A.D. there are expected to be 100 million elderly, about 70% in developing countries. In 1999, 61% of the population of over 60 years age live in developing countries. Meanwhile, in the U.S. 2 million children are looked after by their grandparents (Sial, 1999).

The WHO has classified the SEAR countries as (South East Asian Region: Bangladesh, Bhutan India, Indonesia, Maldives, Myanmar, Nepal, Sri Lanka and Thailand). These countries would have an increased life expectancy. In 1983, 3 of the member states showed a life expectancy at birth of 60 years and more. By 1997, this had been reported by 7 of the member states. In 1980, there were 5.3% elderly reported. By 2025 this was expected to become 12.4% in the SEAR countries. In 1995, the proportion of the elderly population in the SEAR countries was 18.1% of the world total. This was expected to become 21'.4% by 2025 A.D. This was double in population from 1995. By this time, the proportion of males in these countries was expected to be 11.6% , for females 13.2% (Wibowo, 1999).

In the context of this information it is important to have the outlines of a National programme to understand and help the elderly population. This paper is an attempt in this direction.

Background

While the phenomenon of 'ageing' has been widely recognized in developed countries in India during the late 1960s, the Indian Gerontological Association (IGA) with a group of young and enthusiastic scientists from different branches of knowledge has brought this issue to the limelight for academic discussion. According to Lawrence Cohen (2003), "since the 1970s, gerontological writing in India has been dominated by a powerful and seldom challenged narrative of the decline of the Indian joint family and the consequent emergence of old age as a time of difficulty". Prior to industrialization, it was observed that the cultural heritage of Indian society was given the leadership roles and powerful positions of decision-makers and advisors in the joint family and community to aged persons, as their knowledge and experience were considered to be of great value in the proper functioning of society (De Souza 1982; Bhatia 1983; and Mishra 1987). Furthermore, according to Mishra (1987), the technological breakthrough due to industrialization, westernization, and urbanization has neglected the ascribed statuses by weakening the unity and integrity of the joint family and caste group that leads to the negligence of the role and status of the elderly persons. Moreover, the emergences of achieved properties like wealth, education etc., in distorted forms, has colonized the state of mind of the youths by adopting the individualistic value of the West. According to Ambedkar

(1990), the issue relating to old age is a result of the conflict between the traditionalism of the old individuals and the uncritical eagerness of youths towards the Western values (Raju 2002). In fact, there has been a diminishing value of the aged population in contemporary Indian society. As a result, it articulates to the emergence of ageism, which believes in inequality, prejudice and discrimination against aged.

It is against this backdrop that the present paper makes an attempt to understand 'ageing' in India exclusively from a sociological perspective. It also undertakes to outline a brief literature on the existing legislative as well as the policy measures and finally, propose some suggestions towards the future prospect of the elderly individuals of India. The problem of ageing can be seen through the following variables.

Development of Age

Some scholars like Partha N. Mukerji (1972) distinguish between biological and sociological or psychological age. He says, biologically a person may be old, but if he possesses a youthful mentality, sociologically and psychologically speaking, he should be included in the younger generation. Dutt (1986) says, the term ageing signifies the progression of changes in the biochemical processes, which determines structural and functional alterations with age in the cells and non-cellular tissues and, hence, in the whole organism. The prime factors which cause the going process as known today are: environmental; genetic mutation; and free radical theory. He also endorses the view that chronological age is a poor predictor of functional ability. Some 80 years old function as well as the 40 years old and some 40 years old perform life the average 80 years old. While there are no definite criteria fixed by biologists to consider a person old, for administrative purposes each country fixes an age limit, which defines a person as such. The Indian census, for example, has adopted the age of 60 for classifying a person as old.

However we may broadly classify the development of age classes as:

- Era of dependence, socialization and education.
- Era of independence, maturity and responsibility.
- Era of personal fulfillment.
- Potential for self fulfillment in terms of positive as well as negative freedom and responsibility.
- Era of elderly ageing: to be further divided into two types:

(i) The effective elderly (60-75 years), also called young old.

(ii) And elderly in need (above 75 years), called old.

Sociology of Ageing in India: Perspective and Policy Options

The root metaphor of our Indian cultural heritage has been eroding from the Indian soil due to various processes such as: westernization, urbanization and industrialization – in a single word, modernization. Families have instigated to break up, and social support and respect for the elderly is in constant decay. At this juncture, the scientific understanding of this issue is a compulsory task for the academicians as well as the development practitioners.

The multifarious dimensions of ageing in India can sociologically be thought to be a series of transition from one set of social roles to another and such roles are structured by the social system. According to Bhatia (1983), "age and ageing are equally related to role-taki9ng, value orientations and modes of behaviour of a person the expectation of which varies at different age-stages of members of a society". It may be mentioned that the process of ageing is not uniform for all individuals in the society. Thus, a change in the life of the old age, which is considered to be the sanyas ashram of the Hindu ashram theory, is influenced by the biological as well as the social and cultural systems. However, in recent times, the status and role of the old age population have been diminished due to the technological developments that have colonized the outlook of the youths. While contemplating on the issue of the 'aged', the ideas that haunt our imagination are quite complex as well as intriguing. Some argue that the elderly individuals are in a state of 'decay'. It implies that their role in society seem to be redundant and obsolescent for our contemporary times. In other words, they rarely have any function/role to contribute to our times. On the other hand, it is also believed that elderly persons are the guardians of our generation, preservers of the joint families, foundation of experience and knowledge, and resource of traditional values, norms and cultural practices. Thus, at this juncture, sociologists should be engaged in this debate in providing sociological perspectives on the transitional state of affairs of the elderly persons and advocate alternative approaches also for their emancipation to mainstream life.

The Sociological Turn

It seems the discipline of sociology has been almost insouciant to the category called the aged. The 'aged' is about a vulnerable population, which is usually overlooked in our discipline; it is about a population, which is always at risk. No wonder, sociology has been enriching itself by encompassing and integrating new domains of discourse from time to time. From ecology to the Dalits, youth to feminism, though interrelated, it is constantly renewing itself. That is, perhaps the precise attribute of sociology for which August Comte called it a 'dynamic sociology'. Thus, the central methodological question that still remains unresolved is: should sociology make an attempt to construct a discourse for the aged, which would address all the issues confronting the aged? It goes without saying that the literature available on "ageing" in our discipline is very sparse. Thus, perhaps it becomes a methodological imperative for sociologists to build up a systematic discourse on gerontology for a panoptic understanding: their crisis, contribution as well as problems and possibilities. Of late, Social Gerontology, a branch of Gerontology, has started to focus on ageing from the socio-cultural aspects.

A Social Process

Ageing is a by-product of physical, psychological and social processes. While contextualising the process of ageing, the main thrust of the sociology, both as a discipline and a movement, is to reflect on how and to what extent transformations in the society and of the individual life influence each other, as individuals of different age categories pass through social system-institutions, values and norms. Sociologists specify three interrelated processes of ageing: physical, psychological and social. First, the physical ageing refers to the internal and external physiological changes that take place in the individual body. Second, the psychological ageing is understood as the developmental changes in mental functioning – emotional and cognitive capacities. Third, the social ageing focuses on the changes such as : how individuals are viewed, what individuals expect of themselves, and what is expected of them from others that individuals experience over the various age categories. However, sociologists are paying attention to the socio-economic and cultural antecedents of the process of ageing. Furthermore, ageing does not mean what an individual is able to act rather it facilitates what he/she is expected to act, permitted to act or prohibited from acting.

Sociological Perspectives on Ageing

One of the branches of sociology i.e. Sociology of Gerontology or Social Gerontology focuses on what it means to age in society; that is, personal concerns and social issues associated with ageing and the ways in which these themes are influenced and at the same time influence the society in which we life. Thus, according to the sociologists and other social scientists, ageing, looking through the lens of sociological imagination, as devised by C. Wright Mills is not an individual problem rather a widespread issue that is faced by both the developed and underdeveloped nations as a whole. The process of ageing can be approached from four distinct perspectives: functional, symbolic, conflict, and emancipation.

First, the functional perspective argues that the elderly persons having knowledge, wisdom and experience help in the continuation of social norms, values and traditions. Hence, negligence of aged individuals needs to be rectified, according to the social situations. For example, the case of National Agricultural Technology Project (henceforth NATP), which has been initiated by the Ministry of Agriculture, Government of India with the financial assistance from the World Bank and is running with the assistance of the National Institute of Agricultural Extension Management (MANAGE), Hyderabad, in 28 districts covering seven States: Andhra Pradesh, Bihar, Jharkhand, Himachal Pradesh, Maharashtra, Orissa and Punjab. The project aims at mobilization and organization of different farmers' or women farmers' groups at grassroots levels in order to develop and disseminate various agro-based technologies to the farmers'/ women farmers' interest groups (Mishra 2004). It has been observed that although the youths participate in a large number, the aged persons, however, occupy the advisory-cum-central positions at grassroots, block and district levels. The reason is that the youths consider the aged members as more experienced and efficient than them in the concerned field.

Secondly, the conflict perspective assumes that the ageing is problematic for the society. According to this perspective, as the individuals become aged, it leads to the diminishing of power, prestige and privileges, unless these have been maintained by himself or herself. It argues that the wealthy and powerful individuals have blocked efforts to help the aged because they think spending for aged does not serve their personal interest.

Moreover, it points out that the aged individuals, in course of time, lose their memory power and physical strength; thus, their role should be minimized. For example, the case of Yuva, one of the Bollywood block busters of 2004, directed by Mani Ratnam, lays down the significance of youths in the present day Indian politics. The central crux of the movie portrays that the youths must join politics, if the Nation has to survive and prosper. And, finally, the movie ends with its expected slogan. The youths have started taking the power from the hands of the aged. Particularly those who have involved in corruption. But, the sociologically significant question is how the youths perceived politics and students' movements in the contemporary scenario. What I do believe is, that politics and students' movements are positively correlated. Critically examining, the youths want to redefine the knowledge system in relation to the students' movements and politics both at the level of educational institutions and at the level of the State.

Thirdly, the symbolic perspective examines the symbols and definitions that people use to communicate with one another, symbols that provide people with their view of the world. According to this perspective, all individuals with their features and characteristics, which are the reflections of their age, become the symbol of their respective age groups for others. Generally, the youths are considered to be smart, courageous and sportive. On the other hand, as Henslin (1990) mentioned that old persons are seen as weak, indolent, calm et. Thus, we tend to perceive both others and ourselves according to the symbols our culture provides.

Fourthly, the emancipation perspective is an alternative to above three perspectives for two reasons. First, it abandons the approaches, proposed by the above theoretical perspectives. And, secondly, it gives priority to the liberation of the aged from the exclusion of social, economic and political participation in the society. In fact, the emancipation perspective is defined as creation of a sense of social identity of aged in one extreme, and, an instigate to social, economic, political welfare of the aged individuals on the other extreme. In essence, the emancipation perspective provides relative privilege in socio-economic, political and psychological aspects of aged through the construction of a sense of age consciousness, which leads to the provision of social security.

Definitional Problems and Conceptualisations

Different definitions and conceptualizations of ageing have been employed by scholars from time to time, usage of the term 'Elderly' is common both in popular and academic discourses. The use of such blanket term to encompass a forty year range has contributed to the popular stereotype that the elderly constitute a homogeneous social group: one of the most persistent and potent images of ageing is that all older people are alike.

Old age denotes a specific stage of life in a tripartite division of the life cycle, i.e. phase of preparation, followed by the one of productive activity in economic/income generating terms, and finally the stage of retirement. The chronological criterion for classifying an individual or a collectivity as "aged" or "elderly" is generally employed for administrative purposes for example, pensions, retirement, insurance and the like. Here, old age is identified by the transition from the salaried work to retirement.

No definite criterion is fixed by biologist to consider a person old, and for administrative purpose each country tends to carry its age limit for working. The definition of the term "elderly" or "aged" has undergone modification over the passage of time. Ancient Chinese scholars delineated seven phases in a man's life and Pythagoras in the sixth century B.C. compared human life to the seasons. In both cases, old age was deemed to be beyond 60 years (Stub, 1982). Some societies still treat 40 or 50 years as marking the transition into old age.

In Western industrialized nations the typical onset of old age is reckoned as 65. Worach – Kardas (1982) argues that age must be viewed as a socio-cultural category as much as it is a chronological and biological phenomenon, and advocates a life-course perspective in which youth, middle age, and old age are studied as separate entities with their own distinctive problems and processes.

Dutt (1986) says the term ageing signifies the progression of changes in bio-chemical processes. The factors, which cause the ageing process, are mainly environmental, genetic, mutation and free radical theory. Dutt endorses the view that the chronological age is a poor predictor of functional ability. The age of 60 has been adopted by the census of India for the purpose of classifying a person as old.

Old age is determined by cultural norms prevailing in society. In Indian society, marriage of one's children, particularly of a son, heralds the beginning of old age for women far more clearly than do a specified number of years. Accordingly, role expectations change for male and female members in a household.

Old age is depicted positively in terms of wisdom and the potential for spiritual growth. For some, wisdom and serenity are positive aspect of old. The best things about old age include freedom to do and to be what one wishes, i.e. freedom from responsibility and freedom from worry about other's opinions. The "elderly" or "aged" sustain positive self-concepts by narrowing their social contacts to avoid exposure to people who would reject them on account of ageing.

On the other hand, old age is also depicted negatively in terms of physical decline and decrepitude. Elderly people are characterized or stereotyped as ill, tired, mentally slow, self pitying, unhappy and unproductive. They are often depressed by feelings of loneliness and alienation. The negative content of the conditions of old age derives from the relationship of individuals and society; the absence of a role, the isolation from the significant social life, the marginality in family relationship and the lack of commitment, partly induced, partly forced on old people. Their problems include a feeling of material insecurity or dependence, and attenuated intergenerational relationships. The aged are also said to be losing gradually their decision-making authority. Elders suffer from a sense of dispossession that reflects loss of roles and status, as they are deprived of the earlier identities defined by parental or employment functions. The hardest part of being old is declining health and lack of finances, threat of dependence, and the loss of beloved ones.

The Myth of the Aging Mind

One of the most devastating of all myths is the one that predicts that all older persons will gradually lose capacity of their thought processes. The myth also says that older persons think more slowly and more sloppily than do young persons and the intellectual performance of older persons are expected more to slow down (Schwartz & Peterson, 1979).

As revealed from the study and the theoretical discussion the myths about old age are deep rooted in the society and hence it lead to negative attitudes towards the elderly. The elderly are treated as unwanted, non-productive, dependent and dysfunctional, not contributing to the progress or development of society due to afore said myths, misconceptions and wrong notions.

The potential among the elderly is not being realized or utilized by the society due to lack of understanding and dearth of research on this particular aspect. There is need for further research on the societal attitude towards elderly and dissemination of knowledge among the public by educating the families and the community for developing health and positive attitudes towards the aged. Moreover the governmental and non-governmental organizations may take necessary steps for providing institutional and non-institutional services for bringing out the potential among the senior citizens and avail their expertise for the benefit of the society besides taking care of their economic, social and health needs and enabling them to contribute their mite to the society. Social work is probably the most appropriate professional medium to usher efforts in this direction.

2

Plight of Old Aged in India

Traditional Approach

India encompasses within its geographical boundaries an amazing member of ethnic, Linguistic and culturally diverse groups. In addition to Hindu, Muslim, Christian and other Religious groups, there are innumerable Caste groups within the Hindu-fold. Nearly 80 per cent of the people live in rural areas and tribal belts. Of the remaining 20 per cent who live in urban areas, a sizeable section lives in slums, shanty towns. A majority of the Indians is poor and illiterate. The economic activities of the rural tribal people are based predominantly on agriculture, forest resources, some of them are engaged in craft, trading and other forms of traditional economic activities. No doubt the cultural practices and beliefs affect the attitudes of the rural people towards the aged, but the influence of the economic factor is crucial. It is important to note that although the country is poor, there are many rich and upper middle class people. The total number of senior citizens belonging to more affluent sections of the society is, perhaps, more than the total population of many smaller European nations.

The elderly members are respected in all countries in their family and held in high esteem in their community. The aged have a special place in South Asia, especially in the Hindu Community which is predominant in India and Nepal. Deference to old age is a basis on which Hindu society has sought to build up a social order with its characteristic pattern of values, discipline and social organization. This ideal of social order which recognizes the social value of old age is expressed in cultural practices in everyday life. It is inseparable from Varnashram Dharma—the ethico-social order of the Hindu community. This perception of old age is expressed in Hindu mythologies, in fact the entire Vedic heritage of learning had been transmitted down the ages in a teacher - disciple tradition. Vedic seers (rishis) and the first singer - composers of vedic hymns are considered as people endowed with age and wisdom and pictured with streaming silver-white beards. Some of those rishis are claimed to be the founding ancestors of the lineages (gotra and pravara) of the twice-born castes with whom an unbroken connection is genealogically established. A Hindu householder, as part of his daily worship, is obliged to offer oblations to the ancestors of his family and thus the concept of continuity and tradition becomes closely associated with respect and veneration of age. Old age as an event is marked by social and religious celebrations.

In rural India, village elders used to play an important role in the community, there were village panchayats, a body of five persons elected on the basis of their prestige and age. They settled disputes and took decisions which affected the life of the village community. These informal organizations appear to have functioned in a far more institutionalized way in ancient and medieval India and Nepal. The social norms values and code of conduct prescribed in the scriptures and sacred texts, and as they have evolved through the ages, have enjoined the proper authority in the family and community. This is evident even today in some form or the other in rural areas. Although the percentage of aged is small, the senior citizens in India play an important role. In an average Indian household, it is usually the oldest male member of the family who is the head of the household and his decisions are rarely questioned. He owns the property, decides where and how to educate his children, gets his children married when they grow; in fact, he brings under his umbrella, his entire family, regardless of the age of the individual members and considers it his duty to direct, advise and guide them till the moment of his death. The influence of the elderly is far out of proportion to their numbers, in almost every walk of life in India-social, economic and political.

The traditional norms and values of Indian society laid stress on showing respect and providing care for the aged and elderly persons. As a consequence, the aged members of the family were normally taken care of by the family itself. Those who had no family were looked after by the community or caste organizations, through institutions like the sadavarta, dharamshala, muth and the village council or the panchayat. These have been catering to the needs of the aged and the infirm, destitutes in a traditional way.

Indebtedness

Indebtedness is an important economic problem especially in the rural areas. The older persons who are indebted live under great stress and tension (Manider Singh Randhawa, 1991, p.42). In order to find out the indebtedness among the aged respondents they were asked to mention whether they were in debt or not. But a substantial number of widowed (80.8) and divorced/separated elderly (50.0) felt that despite their willingness to take debts from others such as neighbours, friends and known persons others were not interested to give loans or any other lending to the elderly because of the economic inactiveness, economic dependency and lack of source of income and assets. Chi-square test result shows a significant association between marital status and indebtedness.

Table Indebtedness of the Elderly

Marital Status	*Having own house*	*Having own house*	*Total*
Never married	42.9(3)	57.1(4)	100.0(7)
Currently married	35.6(48)	64.4(87)	100.00(135)
Widowed	19.2(30)	80.8(126)	100.0(156)
Divorced/ Separated	50.0(1)	50.0(1)	100.00(2)
Total	27.3(82)	72.7(218)	100.0 (300)

X^2 = 11.11798 ; df: 3; p = 0.0111 (Percentages are row-wise)

The above table shows that 72.7 percent of the aged were having own house while 27.3 percent were not having own house.

Table Quality of life of the Elderly.

Marital Status	*Unsati-factory*	*Satisfactory*	*Very satisfactory*	*Total*
Never married	57.1(4)	28.6(2)	14.3(1)	100.0(7)
Currently married	49.6(67)	48.1(65)	2.2(3)	100.00 (135)
Widowed	67.3(105)	30.8(48)	1.9(3)	100.0 (156)
Divorced/ Separated	50.0(1)	50.0(1)	-	100.00 (2)
Total	59.0(177)	38.7(116)	2.3(7)	100.0 (300)

X^2 = 14.22354; df = 6; p = 0.0272

When aged persons were asked about their life, an overwhelming majority of the aged respondents (59.0) expressed that they were leading unsatisfactory life compared to the 38.7 percent of them who felt their way of living as satisfactory; and only 2.3. percent expressed that they are leading their widowed life very satisfactorily. Among the subjects, those who were widowed (67.3), never married (57.1) and divorced / separated (50.6) also were leading their lives unsatisfactorily which could be due to the fact that they lived alone without anybody's help and did not have anybody to depend upon. The Chi-square test result also shows a significant association between marital status and levels of satisfaction in life.

In the Indian context, aged who are not getting any income have to depend upon their children to fulfill their necessities. They have to face economic and psychological tensions in the family. As aged parents, they too have certain social obligations like attending marriages, deaths of their kin, giving gifts to their married daughters at the time of their visits and so on. Without any income and assets, the aged parents cannot meet these social obligations and further they feel guilty to ask for financial help from their children. The larger proportion of aged is living below the poverty line. The plight of the widowed and divorced/separated elderly is all the more hopeless in this regard. (Vijaya Kumar, 1991, p. 80).

The National Situation

6% of the elderly population lives alone or with non-relatives (Van Willigen; 2000:28). In 1951, the above 60 years population was 20 million (About 5.4% of the total population). By 1991, this became 57 million (6.7% of the total population). This figure included the state of Jammu and Kashmir where no census could be taken. By 1995, this figure was 67.2 million. A Helpage India National Survey of Old Age Homes showed 12,702 residents all over India in the same year. This number was increasing. There was a National shortage of beds. The availability of beds was higher in the South. In 1996, the number was, however, found to be 60 million. By 2001, this number was argued as being between 71-76 million consisting of about 7.7% of the population. By 2016 this was supposed to be between 113-114 million consisting of about 8.9% of the population (Srivastava, 2000).

By 2000 A.D., an estimated 60 and above population 77 million consisting of about 7.6% of the population would exist. This would consist of 7.1% of the total male population and 8.2% of the total female population. Between 1995-2000 the life expectancy was estimated as 62.3 years for males and 62.9 years for females. By 2025 A.D., the older population is estimated to become 168 million, about 12.7% of the total population. While in 2000, the population of those for females. By 2025 A.D., the older population is estimated to become 168 million, about 12.7% of the total population. While in 2000, the population of those who were 80 years and above was 11% of the total for the aged; by 2025 this became 25% as longevity increased. This older population in 2025 included 11.9% of the total males and 13.4% of the total females. Between 2020 and 2025, the life expectancy was expected to be 68.8 years for males and 72.1 for females. By 2050, this older population is expected to become 326 million or about 21.3% of the total population. This is expected to be a higher life expectancy of females. Between 2045 and 2050, the life expectancy was expected to be 73 years for males and 76.9 years for females. The gender gap affects the males adversely (Bose, 2000).

Between 1951 and 1961, the decadal growth rate of the 60 years and above population was 26%. The decadal growth rate of the total population for the same period was 21.6%. Between 1981 and 1991, the decadal growth rate of the 60 years and above population was 31.3%. The decadal growth rate of the total population for the same period was 23.9% (Bose, 2000).

During the 1991 census, it was found that there were 22.2 million 60 years and above workers in India., including 17.8 million males and 4.4 million females. Therefore, 39.1% of the total 60 years and above population were workers. The male workforce participation rate was 60.5%. The female workforce participation rate was 16.1%. The elderly workforce in 9 industrial categories of the census are: cultivators (55.9%), agricultural labourers (22.4%), livestock, forestry, etc., (1.6%), mining and quarrying (0.2%), manufacturing, etc., in households industry (2.4%), manufacturing, etc., in other than household industry (3.9%), construction (1.0%), trade and commerce (6.6%), transport, etc. (0.9%) and other services (5%). 78% of the elderly workforce is engaged in agricultural activities. 84% of the female elderly workforce is engaged in agricultural activitites (Bose, 2000).

In 1995-96, the 52nd Round of the National Sample Survey showed that among elderly rural males, 48.5% claimed non-dependence on others, 18% were partially dependent and 31.3% were fully dependent. Among elderly rural females, 70.6% were fully dependent on others. 14.6% were partially dependent and 12.1% were not dependent on others. Among the elderly urban males, 51.5% were not dependent on others, 29.7% were fully dependent on others and 16.9% were partially dependent. Among elderly urban females, 75.7% were fully dependent on others, 11% were partially dependent and 11.5% were not dependent on others (Bose, 2000).

Over 75% of the economically dependent elderly are supported by children and grand children. Children support 73.2% of the rural males and 76.5% of the urban males. Grandchildren support 4.8% of rural males and 5.2% of the urban males. Among elderly females; children support 69.9% of rural females and 67.9% of urban females. Grandchildren support 5.2% of the rural females and 5.5% of urban females (Bose, 2000).

In the ages of 60-69 years there are 46.3% widows, in between 70-79 years there are 66.1% widows and in the years of 80 or above, there are 69.8% widows. In 1991, the total number of widows of 60 years or above are 14.8 million. The total number of widowers was 4.5 million (Bose, 2000).

In 1901, there were 12 million elderly amounting to 5.1% of the total population. By 1990, this became 57 million. It is expected to exceed a 100 million by 2013. By 2050, this is expected to become 21%. At the age of 65 years or above it is 3.4% or 30 million in number (Joshi and Sengupta, 2000).

The National Sample Survey Organization in 1991 found 45% of the elderly to be suffering from chronic illnesses. 70% of the elderly in the urban areas and 34% in rural areas were found to be economically dependent. 6% of the elderly in the urban areas and 8% in the rural areas lied only (Joshi and Sengupta, 2000). This has been emphasized by these authors:

"In a developing country like India, the elderly people suffer from the dual medical problems of both communicable as well as degenerative disease. This is further confounded by impairments of special sensory functions like vision and hearing. The elderly are highly vulnerable to infections diseases because of a decline in their immune functions and atrophic changes in various organs. The physiological changes in the old age lead to impaired cough reflex, impaired circulation and tissue perfusion. There is deficient collagen synthesis and poor wound healing. Further, incidence of infection remains high because of poor nutrition and high intake of immuno suppressive drugs". (Joshi and Sengupta, 2000:42).

Further, pneumonia is 50 times more common in elderly than in adolescents and accounts for half the deaths caused due to respiratory diseases, excluding cancer. Urinary tract infections are particularly common among the elderly. A symptomatic bacteriurea affects 30% of elderly women and 7% of elderly men. The common cause of urinary tract infections in the elderly is the insertion of the catheter and other instruments. The prevalence of tuberculosis is higher among the elderly than the younger individuals. Chronic illnesses include hypertension, coronary heart disease, diabetes, etc. Hypertension was found to be higher in females, reaching to 323 per thousand in rural areas. Coronary heart diseases were more common in urban areas and was higher for males than for females. Diabetes mellitus was also higher in urban areas, affecting 5 million of the elderly in 1966 (Joshi and Sengupta, 2000).

The incidence of cancer was higher in both elderly males and females as compared to the total population. In 1996, the total number of elderly with cancer was 0.35 million, prostate cancer being the commonest malignancy in males. The chance of males of over 50 years of age contracting this disease in 30% and their mortality is 25%. The crude prevalence rate of stroke or cardio-vascular disease is 200 for every 1,00,000 persons. It is caused by hypertensionl tobacco usage; obesity and diabetes mellitus. Cataract is the most common cause of blindness among the elderly in India. 1.5% of the elderly are blind, a majority of them from rural areas. The WHO in 1989 found 12 million Indians to be blind and in need of eye-care services (Joshi and Sengupta, 2000).

It was also found that fruits, leafy green vegetables and milk are rarely consumed in adequate amounts. A belief existed that such expensive items should be given to the younger people (Joshi and Sengupta 2000; Srivastava, et al., 1996).

Cardiovascular disorders account for 1/3rd of the mortality among the elderly. Respiratory disorders cause 10% of the mortality while infections and tuberculosis account for another 10%. Neoplasm accounts for 6% and accidents, poisoning and violence constitute less than 4% of the elderly mortality with similar rates for nutritional, metabolic, gastro-intestinal and genito-urinary infections. 4 million elderly persons of 60 years or above are mentally ill. 2/3rd of their mental morbidity consists of affective disorders, especially depression and late onset of psychosis, while 1/3rd is dementia (Ray, 1994; Joshi and Sengupta,2000).

3. Improving Support Systems in India

In America, Senior Citizens' Centres have come up all over the country, providing a variety of services. Voluntary organizations and government agencies work hand in hand to organize support programmes for the care of the aged. In India it is necessary to draw up a plan of action and implement it. This would be a better way of helping senior citizens than advise and lip sympathy, or the offer of dole which they may detest, because no so long before they were able-bodied respectable citizens winning bread for their families and looking after themselves with respect and dignity. Hence the task of helping the aging is delicate because the recipients of help are very sensitive. The programmes to assist the aging can be achieved through:

- Cooperation from the family with its aging members
- Counselling from the society with senior citizens centres offering guidance on all matters.
- Help from the government, special amenities and concessions and
- The ageing helping themselves.

Since family continues to be the unit for their care and the elderly generally live with one or more of their children or other close relatives, ability of the family to cope with their physical, financial, psycho-social, recreational and other needs should be strengthened through supportive social services. Since the most satisfactory form of care of the aging continues to be the one that makes possible the stay of the elderly with their children, policies and programmes should facilititate this as extensively as possible. There has to be a greater attempt at orienting family members to the needs of the old and of the ways in which they can prevent them from feeling neglected and ensure their participation, involvement and consultation on different matters. Elderly people, too need to be educated about their changing role due to the stress of modern living and the contribution that they can and should make rather than adopt the traditional Indian-role of only receiving attention.

The elderly must be helped to remain in their homes and accustomed surroundings for as long as possible. This demands properly organized social services, decentralized medical care and access to other facilities. Community should introduce a set of measures which would help in strengthening the family through supportive actions so that most of the aged are taken care of within the family itself. Lack of financial resources has been felt to be a major hurdle. Keeping in view the present demographic and social trends in the country, there does not seem to be any escape from the need for introducing a uniform social security scheme of pension, or financial assistance, to provide succour to the aged. This is an imperative need if a realistic and integrated view of development is taken, specially involving family welfare. Investment in social security, particularly in relation to familial welfare is also an investment in other aspects of family welfare.

There is an urgent need for succour to the old with the meager income of most of the families to which these old people belong and with the rising cost of living everyday. In order to have some monetary relief to the family it is necessary to give some financial help to the old. Any help of this kind alone is not going to solve the problem. Since accommodation in the house is equally important under the present set-up, in big towns and cities, home of the aged or senior citizens in some form or the other has become a must.

Day care centres will be of great service to the elderly, especially in metropolitan cities on account of shortage of living space. The centres need to be organized in different neighbourhoods and provide for social and group activities like talks, discussions, entertainment, community services, training for income generation, visit of potential employers, doctors, legal experts, financial experts, counselors, politicians and others. Religious practices play an important part in supporting the aged. The centres, therefore, make provisions for prayer meetings, satsanga, meditation, yoga practices, bhajans and kirtans. As one ages, one turns sensitive and emotional in approach and expects the people around to respect him/her for the accumulated experience. Humiliation and suffering encountered by seniors make them depressed and frustrated of their very existence at the fag end of their life. Even an elderly neighbour living on his own, alone, needs love, respect and affection. A courtesy call once in a while and invitation to visit and spend sometime in the company of elderly make them feel elated and that the society has not rejected him/her. It is the compassion and affectionate torch of the fellow human beings that give moral support to the aged and inculcate a sense of satisfaction in their existence in society. The service centres can undertake the activities like home visits, counselling and helping the home bound aged in their day-to-day requirements. Such centres should be managed by senior citizens who are interested in taking up jobs. Intensive training should be organized for them to manage the centres on commercial basis.

Service centres for the aging can play a twin role. They can aim not only at harnessing the economic and social potential of the aging by utilizing their skills and experience but also seek to provide a wide range of services to cater to their needs. The aging can provide succour and relief to the sick, the disabled and the destitute and also contribute to economic and social development.

Of late, there has been a growing recognition of the need to pay attention to developing the potential of the aging because, with raising standards of nutrition and medical care, not only is the proportion of the aging in the population increasing but there is also an upgrading of their health status and physical capacity for a continuing active life. The aging are active and able to care for themselves. They are not a spent force or an unproductive burden on society. There is a general desire on the part of the aging themselves to play a productive role in society and to ensure that their knowledge and ability are fully recognized. The aging constitutes an important resource which may nations are grossly underutilizing at present.

The socio-economic survey conducted in Delhi on behalf of the Citizenship Development Society showed that service centre for the aged should work in an integrated and coordinated manner as there is a high degree of complementarity between different units. It should have representatives from the local community and make a sustained effort to ensure its participation. The centre can be started in a rented building to start with; later it can acquire its own land and building. A small fee can be charged for its services except from the indigent. The centre with its full complement and services may develop by stages depending on the preferences of the donors and the priorities of the client group. Since space or built up places are not easily available in many cities even on rental basis, it is worth examining whether some corners in public parks or school premises can be used as short-term measure to launch the programmes.

Day care centres certainly provide the necessary support to caregivers and keep the aged in the family setting. They help the elderly to spend a few hours during day time, fruitfully in the company of their peer group. It is worth examining whether night care centres can also be set up for the needy aged.

When the respondents were asked whether their advices were followed by their children or not, a substantial percentage of elderly (69.3%) claimed that their advices were not valued.

Table : Validity of Decisions

Marital status	*Decisions not valid*	*Decisions valid on*					*total*
		Agriculture	*Children's Issues*	*Religious issues*	*Business issues*	*Others*	
Never married	85.7(6)	-	-	-	-	14.3(1)	2.3(7)
currently married	52.6(71)	41.5(56)	3.7(5)	0.7(1)	0.7(1)	0.7(1)	45.0(135)
Widowed	82.7(129)	9.6(15)	5.8(9)	0.6(1)	-	1.3(2)	52.0(156)
Divorced/ Separated	100.0(2)	-	-	-	-	-	0.7(2)
Total	69.3(208)	23.7(71)	4.7(14)	0.7(2)	0.3(1)	0.3(4)	100.0(300)

$X^2 = 54.84447$; df = 15;p = 0.0000 (Percentages among categories are row-wise and among totals are table-wise.)

Many elderly persons claimed that their advices on agriculture were followed by their advises on religious issues (0.7%), business (0.3%) and others (0.3%) were valued respectively. It is observed from the study that opinions of most of the 'never married' (85.7) and 'widowed' elderly were not valued by their children due to social myths which are ascribed to the old age persons with advancing age. The Chi-square test value shows a highly significant association between marital status and validity of decisions. However, the data also evidences that, in varying proportions, others still utilize the advices and decisions of elderly in various areas.

Ageing in India: Some Reflections

The aged population in India is currently the second largest in the world. In modern times, for all practical purposes the individuals who are above sixty years of old are considered to be aged or 'senior citizens' of the State. In academic research, retirement age is often taken as an index of aged status. Chronological age of fifty eight or sixty is considered the beginning of old age. However, existence of mass poverty, growing trends towards nuclear family greater life expectancy and deterioration of cultural values and norms are engendering stumbling blocks on the part of the aged to cope with the changing environment (Bhatia 1983). As a result, the aged population in India is accompanied by a series of problems in their day-to-day life. The major areas of problems, faced by the aged individuals are: income generation, health, use of free time, social security, social participation, dignity and respect and so on. These problems are because of the following reasons namely, geographical and cultural differences, red-tapism and disproportionate socio-economic facilities to urban and rural areas in terms of education, sanitation, health and housing. As a result, the Government of India has undertaken some legislative and policy measures for the welfare of the aged.

Existing Programmes on Ageing

Much progress has been made in the quality and quantity of the service of the ageing in India in the last five decades. However, improvements have been uneven in the urban areas that avail the best advantage of modern advanced technological package in contrast to the rural one. While much of the emphasis has been given to care for women and a child, the government has played a least role for aged except formulating certain legislative and policy measures. Here, a brief attempt has been made to understand the constitutional and the legislative and the policy measures pertaining to the welfare of the aged population of India.

Constitutuional Provisions

The welfare of the aged has been enshrined in the Constitution of India. The item 9 of the State list and items 20, 23 and 24 of the Concurrent List speak of the provisions of age pension, social security, social insurance, economic and social planning, and relief to the disabled and the unemployed. The Article 41 of the Directive Principles of State Policy expresses "the State shall make effective provision for securing the right to work, to education and to public assistance in case of unemployment, old age, sickness and disableness, and in other cases undeserved wants, within its limits of economic development and capacity". Fundamental Right, Article 16 (2) emphasizes on equal opportunity in matters of public employment. Article 47 of the Indian Constitution points out the raising of the level of nutrition and the standard of living of its people and improvement of public health.

Legislative Measures

Coming to the category of legislative measure, the retirement benefits (GPF & PPF) are provided to those who served the Government and the public undertakings.

- The Employees Provident Funds and Miscellaneous Provisions Act, 1952 (amended in 1996) provide for economic security to persons or their families in the event of retirement or even death before retirement.
- The National Social Assistance Programme came into existence on 15th August 1995 and one of its programmes is the National Old Age Pension Scheme that is implemented through the Panchayats and municipalities. Presently, all State Governments and Union Territories are implementing the old age pension scheme under the State sector.

Policy Measure

The emergence of National Policy on Older Persons,1999, a collaborative pursuit 0of both public and private agencies along with the 'Third Sector', which aims at the well-being of the aged focuses on the areas of financial security, health care and nutrition, shelter, welfare and other needs of the senior citizens and provides protection against abuse and exploitation. Moreover, the National Council for Older Persons on 18th October 2002 and 7th February 2003 emphasizes on the following areas: uniform age of 60+ for extending facilities / benefits to senior citizens; financial security; health care and nutrition needs; food security and shelter; and highlighting the role of media.

However, the empirical implications of the measures through legislation and policy measures have not achieved their desired goals. The result is that the rich used to receive more and perhaps better services than the poor, although the poor are deserving and downtrodden (Hess, Markson and Stein 1998). Moreover, owing to the physical, socio-economic, psychological and the influence of uncritical western philosophy like 'individualism', out of their practical experience and research endeavour, an innumerable number of social scientists report that there is degradation in the social status as well as economic conditions of the aged population in India. In fact, the living conditions of the aged population in India. In fact, the living conditions of the aged individuals in Indian society are influenced by a series of factors such as caste, religion, education, health condition, dependent on the chief earner of the family, living standard of the adult members of the family and the process of migration (Raju 2002 and Mishra 1987). Furthermore, the unconditional power, prestige and privileges that older people used to enjoy in joint families are being gradually eroded in the society. Thus, there is an urgent need for the restructuration of the existing legislative and policy measures.

Reading Future Options

In India, as stated above, the living standards of the aged are influenced by the following factors: physical, social, economic and psychological. Thus, any attempt towards the welfare of the aged community should be taken into consideration the above mentioned factors. Moreover, any policy should include the poor, vulnerable and neglected segments of the society. In a concrete sense, as Farah (2004) mentions, the policy option should recognize the following four objectives:

1. To bring about every individual to an equal and common platform in order to launch any measures and provide equal opportunities for basic amenities like food, shelter, health care facility etc.
2. To provide equal socio-economic opportunities to everybody by removing all sorts of discriminations that operates at societal level.
3. To ensure the institutional and regulatory mechanism for discrimination.
4. To mainstream the marginalized sections of the society.

Here, an attempt has been made to propose some suggestions for the development of the longstanding issue relating to 'ageing' in India. Moreover, these suggestions will act as critical inputs into the process of developing an appropriate policy measure for the welfare of the aged individuals.

- India lives in her villages. Furthermore, Indian economy is primarily an agrarian-based economy. She is characterized by the existence of longstanding variations, such as, rural-urban dichotomy; rich and poor difference; the unequal distribution of updated technological facilities etc. Hence, any proposed measure undertaken by the government should take into account these factors. In this context, the first and foremost thing is that the government should adopt a provision of social security measure irrespective of rural and urban, caste and class so on and so forth. Here, the social security measure believes that the State should make itself responsible for ensuring a minimum standard of material welfare to all its citizens.
- The aged individuals should be encouraged to form Self-Help Groups (SHGs) so that they can organize themselves and to provide services to their fellow senior citizens. Moreover, it will facilitate a sense of 'age consciousnesses among the aged individuals'.
- Apart from the improvement of health care system, the effective way of dealing with the elderly is to improve the economic condition of the elderly population. Thus, there is a need to formulate an alternative employment opportunity for the aged; at least those who have efficiency to work after retirement, whereby they can increase their bargaining power in contemporary competitive society.
- In recent times, the process of 'participation' seems to be the buzzword in every sphere of intellectual discourse. Thus, along with the youth, the aged need to participate instead of staying in isolation in all the communitarian or societal or development activities. This participation is

expected to bring about the developments of equality, efficiency and effectiveness, which ultimately lead to mainstream life.

- There is also a need to revive our normative structure of the society. Owing to the influence of distorted form of modernity, the philosophy of 'individualism' has colonized the mental state of the youths. Thus, efforts should be promoted in order to tackle this situation.
- There is also a need to introduce the institutional support in order to address the structural problem of ageing. This institutional sep up will deliver training programmes, oriental course, and mass campaign against the attitude towards ageism. On the other hand, it will also conduct various research works pertaining to the problems relating to ageing and will also find out the possible solutions.
- Advocacy, research, involvement of voluntary agencies, training opportunities for gerontological workers, awareness building and a close networking between the old aged population with the national and international agencies should also be developed.
- Finally, the emergence of collaborative effort made by the public and private agencies along with the 'Third Sector' and also the public at large will address effectively the conditions of ageing. This multi-agential strategy is based on interactive-bottom up approach and active participation of stakeholders.

Indian Elderly and Various Role Situations

In India studies show that the family is the prime source of social economic and emotional support for the elderly and the first line of support for physical care. It has often been observed that care of the elderly depends upon the status and prestige enjoyed by time in the family. This status depends on several factors viz., the material possession and physical ability to share the family burden. This status in turn becomes the factor to decide ones well being and care in the family. Any dereliction in the duty of the elderly will severe the marimonial relation in the family with other members in no time.

Well being of the elderly depends on the nature and extent of factors such as role erosion, role overload, role isolation, role expectation conflicts etc., (Bali, 1999), besides personal and resources inadequacy.

Roles Overload

It leads to stress and strain as well as fatigue, both physically and psychologically as well as economically and socially for elderly, particularly in cases of women. The elderly women are bound by various domestic changes and other economic activities in her youth and supplementing the family income in their middle age. Besides, care young and old members of the family. Due to onset of age and other physical vagaries it becomes too demanding for them to comply with all sorts expectation, at the twilight hours of their life by younger family members. This also sometimes have deleterious effects on their mental and physical health.

Role Isolation

Role isolation occurs when an individual particularly an elderly, feels isolated from the channels of communication or is being kept out our side lined or not being part of what is happening. Being displaced, sidelined from their earlier position of importance, advice sought and key decision maker within the family one matter of vital importance, could have serious consequences on their well-being. This could lead to loneliness and boredom. Perceived non-usefulness causes a lot of unhappiness. This problem is much severe in widow, separated or divorced or in cases or desertion.

Role Expectation

Every individual in a family has certain ascribed role by virtue of being born or being part of a particularly family, so they are to play a set of defined roles. At times roles players subjects himself to an evaluation in keeping with his or her own expectations the role being played. In the event there is perceived conflict in the role expectations then this is likely to have bearing on the well being of the elderly. This could arise when the elderly expects a certain kind of level of help or care but is not forthcoming. Such situation can affect the elderly aversely.

Role Conflict

Role expectation conflict could arise between the elderly and other primarily due to differences in the perception and the values attached to the performance of the roles. Recognition of this indicates and fact that conflicting needs and desires of the elderly and other cannot possibly be fulfilled due to various limitations.

The various role sets as describes are purely the produced of culture and its change over a period of time due to modernization and urbanization combined with industrialization. The study of role sets are important as the socio-cultural dimension of the process of modernization and urbanization is incomplete without it, in case of emerging population of peoples aged 60 years and above.

Population Aging

Over the past fifty years, mortality rates have declined in developing countries raising the average life span from around 41 years in 1950 to almost 62 years in 1990. According to WHO, this average life span is expected to reach 70 years by 2020. One of the main features of the world population in the 20th century has been a phenomenal increase in the elderly population in both the developed and developing countries. Approximately among the 580 million elderly (60 years and above) in the world, around 355 million live in developing countries. The number of elderly world wide by 2020 is expected to cross 1000 million with over 700 million of them in developing countries. The population of those who are 60 and above constituted 5.66 per cent of the total population in 1951 in the case of India. India had 25 million persons over 60 years in 1961 and 33 million in 1971. The figure rose to 40 million in 1981. In 1991, the figure further increased to 56 million constituting 6.5 per cent of the total population. The population of the aged was predicted to become 76 million by 2001, forming 7.6 per cent of population and nearly one-seventh of the world elderly. By 2020, the number may rise to 124 million, which means 11 per cent of the population will be under 15 years. Increase in longevity does increase the aged population, but the concern is how active this populations?

Population ageing has been occurring much faster in developing countries, due to rapid fertility decline and increasing life span through medical interventions, providing effective treatment and prevention of diseases that used to be fatal. Thus rapid growth of ageing population has become a serious challenge to public health globally.

Ageing is a natural process, spanning the life period from conception through Birth—Infancy—Childhood—Adolescence—Adulthood—Old Age to Death. Each of these stages has unique characteristics and vulnerabilities requiring special attention to ensure optimum health during each stage. Concerted efforts are on the agenda to provide for mechanisms leading to active ageing, but translating them into action is the need of the hour.

The Physical and mental health in each stage influences the further stages in life span, which ultimately leads to the active aged population if proper attention is paid for the health care needs of individuals at each stage.

Dramatic influence in medical and health care facilities due to scientific and industrial advancements has brought about an increased longevity for the human race. However improved and advanced may be the achievements in the world of health care, there is no denying the fact that an advancing age and increased longevity are often accompanied by psych-social problems for the elderly. While medical and health care facilities can and do treat bodily afflictions, they do not have solutions to the problems of the mind and soul. Active ageing does not depend only on physical health but also on the psycho-social well being of the individual. Treatment of the mind and the soul requires concerted inputs into addressal of the root causes for emotional upsets, noticeable behavioural changes and difficulty in coping with the stress and strain of advancing age.

Rapidly increasing aged population is one of the biggest political and socio-economic issues in the present day world. The discussion on this issue is problem centred and seems to include several controversial statements. The ageing population is both a threat and a burden but also a great challenge and opportunity. The gerontological theories – whether activity or disengagement oriented, whether functional or critical seem to support this variety and also the discordance of attitudes and visions.

The aim of the present paper is a comprehensive exposition of the ageing question from the point of view of challenge but also of worries: to highlight the societal and cultural pre-requisities and obstacles towards active, successful and healthy ageing. This article is a review of the problems and prospects to understand the multitude of active, successful and healthy ageing. One of the issues that is often taken up, is the age question: generations and age cohorts are seen in serious confrontation against each other more so than for instance different kinds of families— and it seems that age has became one of the core issues in welfare redistribution.

Accordingly the paper presents the introduction of the concepts of active, successful and healthy ageing and continue the logic of social and cultural capital and deals with the way in which ageing can contribute to development, focusing on the welfare of the aged themselves ending up to ponder their impact on active ageing.

The question then arises: Whether these active elderly who have good education, knowledge and experience in their field of work can contribute to the community and country? If yes, then what and how? Are their any impediments to their being thus utilized? Can some thing be done about it, in case there are preventable drawbacks? If yes, what? If not why? All these are important questions to which the attention is drawn in the ensuing discussion particularly in the area of active, successful and healthy ageing.

3

Social and Health Perspectives of Elderly

Transition of youth to adulthood and thereafter to old age is an imminent natural phenomenon and is a significant outcome of demographic transition. Ageing of population is primarily the result or reductions in fertility and mortality. Ageing of population was first recognized as a matter of concern in the developed countries and which later on become worldwide phenomenon. Among the less developed regions of Asia, Africa and Latin America, it is Asia, which has been the most successful in reducing the growith rate of population. In India since 1961 decline in the overall death rate and also in morality levels in the older age groups initiated a process of ageing. This has since accelerated after 1971 when the fertility level also started declining. According to census of India the post 60 years population increased from 12.06 million in 1901 the number of elderly increased by about 67 per cent, reaching 32.70 million by 1971. During 1971-81 the increase in the aged population was about 32 per cent as against the increase of 24.7 per cent recorded for the total population during this period. During the decade 1981-91 the old age population increased by 13.5 million with a decadal growth rate of 31 per cent. According to estimates made by the Technical Group on Population increased by 13.5 million with a decadal growth rate of 31 per cent. According to estimates made by the Technical Group on Population Projections, the likely number of the elderly by the year 2016 will be around 113 million. It is, therefore, clear that the India population of aging brought on by a decline in fertility in better opportunities for survival.

Ageing of population refers to the increasing proportion of old people in the total population of a nation. Fertility and mortality are the key biological factors in the process of ageing. The combination of high mortality and fertility rates results in a population with large group of young people. Gradual decline in the level of mortality, the proportion of young people declined and the increased. The decline in the levels of fertility and morality invariably result in increase in the proportion of adult people in the population. As the population passes through traditional society to urbanized and industrialized modern society, demographic transition takes place which leads to shifts in the age structure and reduces the proportion the young people coupled with increase in the proportion of reduces of the proportion of the young people coupled with increase in the proportion of old age population. Due to low mortality and fertility rate population grows ageing.

For a variety of reasons ageing has not yet become an issue for serious consideration in India. Perhaps because of a preoccupation with the problems of a massive child and youth population, or perhaps Indian society still maintains a rather strong family system which provides social security for elders. The spread of education industrialization combined with a considerable number of the offspring of the elderly moving away to other areas in search of employment and a dynamic family structure in the villages and cities of India there are obvious social commitments to be taken care of for elderly care in the years to come.

Ageing Some Socio Economic Issues

Dr. Kumudini Dandekar in her book "The elderly in India" (1996) has gone into various psychosocial facts of elderly and ageing in India population. She quoted anthropologists, Corninne N. Nydegger (1985:406) who describes three myths showing how an average person looks at the problem of aging. One is the 'golden age of the past' from which modern man has fallen, most often as a consequence of his own sinful acts. The historian Laslett (in Nydegger, 1985:407,411) has called this the 'world we have lost' syndrome. The second myth is that of the 'golden island' where things run smoothly as far as the old are concerned. The third is the idea of the 'rosy family'. It is a nuclear family with an intergenerational network that provides strength, love and sustenance in all its members" (1996). Further she added that the ageing is intrinsic to one and all and it is reactive as well.

The Old and Physical - Social Changes

The aging effect resulting from industrialization and its accompaniments are of two kinds: intrinsic and reactive. Intrinsic affects are due to biological changes with aging. Reactive effects arise from social structures including the family structure, which itself is the result of industrialization and other changes. Most old age behaviour is reactive in the sense that it is shaped by social experience. For instance, modernization affects the whole life cycle, with changes in longevity, health's standards, medication, age at marriage, age at retirement, economic circumstances, social security, etc. These affected the attitudes to old age. The obvious process of modernization and industrialization for any developing country including that of India interplayed with the family structure and the people more so with the elderly

The process of modernization and industrialization in India has definitely impact on the elderly population. Their worldview towards their own family and society has changed remarkably scholars like Dandekar had defined the issue in a subtle and comprehensive manner. Adopting a micro approach to the elderly, their problems may be viewed from the perspective of individual satisfaction. Some scientists have suggested two kinds of theories to view individual cases the activity theory and disengagement theory. Activity theory is concerned with the extent to which the old continue their activities of middle age. Disengagement theory can be seen as the opposite of activity theory, concerned as it is with the reasons and consequences of disengagement. The old invariably disengage themselves at various ages, which is good for both the individuals and society.

With the transition of society from the agricultural to the industrial stage, there was a shift from agricultural practice in a bid way and change in the setting of old was to follow. In an agrarian set up, each member of the household has the same source of income. In an industrialized society, on the other hand, an individual wage earner makes for difficulties in budgeting because of the different sources of income available. Instead of being a productive unite providing for all, the household is now a consumer unit, and those who do not earn are likely to be overlooked when their rights of consumption are assessed. In traditional families the older people accepted the burden of providing for the family, and the next generation living with them could enjoy their income if any. But in the non-agricultural context, when the elderly cease to earn they become acutely conscious of their non-earning status and experience a sense of helpless dependency. In urban areas usually it is the old from rural areas that go to live in the son's house. In the urban setting adult children might event take advice from the elderly but might not act on it, knowing that their elderly parents are not sufficiently experienced in the demands of the new setting.

Finally, new standards of behaviour, new ways of spending time and money, and the like provide specific grounds for conflict between generation remains silent, suppressing its feelings of disapproval before the young, it risks being subjects to verbal argument and contradiction. Within their cultural framework, this constitutes the antithesis of appropriate modes of intergenerational communication.

In all the above ways, families, which include older people, are affected by the social transition-taking place in urban India. The impact of changes in the economic structure, geographical mobility, education and cultural values is felt at all economic and social levels. But for the poor, especially poor migrants of recent rural origin, these changes threaten the time-tested system of old age security because aged members of these families have no material power base that can be used to enforce devotion from their offspring in the face of adverse circumstances.

As we have seen, the rural population is being pushed out of an agricultural setting into urban areas. All the companying ills of this transition are further aggravated by poverty. The traditional family may seem strong. It may also perhaps cushion many of the potentially adverse effects of urbanization of the existing social order. But it is a mistake to think that the future of the family is not changing in an Indian cultural context, given the material conditions in which millions of urbanites lived today. It is not easy to say what solutions can be found. But people must be at least aware about what the future has in store for them. Perhaps this is the first step needed to face the new problems.

Ageing Modernization and Role Play

The socio cultural issues those are constantly interplaying with the process of aging can broadly be categorized as change of various rates of the role conflicts among the elderly due to modernizations. Modernization has given a new paradigm to our society and culture. The instrument of metamorphosis is the newer roles played willy nilly by the elderly in our society. The new roles have by the large made the old dependent on the young ones of the family, i.e., the information technology based society with rampant usage of plastic money. Thus the old are getting stressed to cope with the new roles. The coping mechanism is very much a part and parcel of cultural and learning mechanism. And the learning is also a part of life course.

The cultural concept is important in understanding the ageing experience because experience is moulded through cultural. Reality is cognized, cultural is cognition and therefore culture is reality as it is experienced. (Willigen et al, 1999).

Cultural acquisition takes place over a period of time. Cultural traits such as learning teaching and forgetting cultural content occur throughout o0nes lifetime. Cultural ageing and de-acquisition of knowledge with specific ages are quite common. Cessation of learning causes a "cultural necrosis". And such a death causes loss of adaptability, innovation and capacity for change. The cultural age of a person consists of their possessing the knowledge that is expected for a specific period of their life. A conception of cultural age would reflect a person's position in the closely related social dimension; this is some way related to chronological age. (Fry, 1990).

A concept of life course is universalistic across the societies (Riley, 1979). This deals in stages in the life of individual combined with expected code of behaviour. This type life course behaviour is evinced in ancient Hindu scriptures, an ethnological model coupled with a culturally constituted disengagement theory. The Hindu life course is divided into four stage, i.e. (Brahmachayra Student), Girhastha (householder), Vanprashta (hermit) and Sanyas (a renunciate). The conception of ideal life course is more or less diametrically opposed to the ideas associated with activity theory. These theories often tend to reflect the cultural setting in which these are developed. While Havighurst (1963) a proponent of activity theory saw the process of normal aging as maintenance of activities and attitudes of middle age. If one is forced to give a role, thought retirement for example, other roles should be substituted. This point is also endorsed in Protestant ethic, it emphasizes orientation towards work, activity and social responsibility.

Ageing process is an expression of an individual cultural mooring developed by a community, which is non-identical in nature so far as two different communities are concerned. These changes can be conceived in different ways. One way is that social age can be conceived of is as an individuals identity and participation in various age-staged cultural institutions. Similar, concept of social 'ageing would involve passages through the succession of roles and related, norms that exist in particular society.

A Socially Determined Category

Every society uses age categories to divide this ongoing process into stages or segments of life. These life stages are socially constructed rather than inevitable. Age, too, is a production of social category. At any point of life span, age simultaneously denotes not only a number and a mixture of physical characteristics but also a set of social constructs, defined by the norms specific to a given society at a specific point in history. Think about childhood, for example. When you were growing up, childhood was a distinct period of life with particular activities designed especially for your age group: television programmes, movies, school, music etc. Thus, a specific period of life, be it infancy, childhood, adolescence, adulthood, middle age or old age is influenced by the structural entities of a given society. Therefore, ageing is not to be considered the mere product of biological function rather a consequence of socio-cultural factors.

Moreover, what is important about ageing, then, is how a society uses it to put people into categories. As a classificatory tool, age is important in three ways. First, like sex, age is an ascribed status or characteristic, which is, based on attributes over which we have little or no control. Second, unlike sex, a specific age is always transitional – constantly moving from one age to another, beginning life at zero and ending with a certain number at death that is regulated by societal expectations of age-appropriate behaviour. These transitions also assume that conformity is rewarded whereas deviance is punished. Third, although in every society some age groups are more powerful, rich and respectable than others; the unique aspect of ageing is that everyone can expect to occupy various positions throughout life on the basis of his or her age. The equation is very simple – all of us, at certain time, were powerless infants, and in course of time, the power and influence change as we move from one age category to another. Thus, the definition of ageing is socially caused.

Social Networks and the Aged in India

In India, the joint family is not only an entity by itself, but is also an integral part of the social system. It functions in a framework of interlinkages that hold each member of the family within its fold. As a functioning unit within the economy and society, it is the means through which goods are produced and consumed. As the medium for retaining and transmitting land and other movable as well as immovable assets, its stability has been vital to the functioning of the social order. Its intimate relationship with the soil has also been an element in extending these affiliations beyond the simple household to a broad range of other kin brought together by common patrimony.

Social networks, for the purpose of this paper, will include multiple linkage group, the workmates and professional colleagues. The support will depend on the nature, extent and type of crisis. The intensity of feelings may decrease as kin increase distance by blood and marriage to other collateral kin, relations and friends. Spatial propinquity with neighbours and workmates, and professional proximity with colleagues, create a feeling of concern for each other's well-being.

The dependence of the individual on the authorities in India, from birth to adulthood, is at variance with the non-authoritarian approach is Western culture. The opportunities for personal gratification are limited by the concepts of duty towards relations, specially elders. These relationships extend in a circle of social networks consisting of family, kinship and territorial affinities. Social networks provide an excellent mechanism for looking after aged members in the family.

In social networks the family, and specially the joint family, is considered a more significant entity than the individual. It is difficult for the individual to conceive of himself as a person separate from or outside the family. The family system and the caste system lay down the code of conduct for each member; his relationship with others is also determined thereby.

Social organization in the West, and particularly in American society, is dominated by the attribute of husband-wife relationship which shapes the individual-0centred orientation of American culture, which is characterized by self-reliance. On the other hand, Indian social organization is dominated by the father-son relationship and the attributes of this relationship give form to the situation-centred orientation of our culture, expressed in the shape of mutual interdependence. These varying patterns of psycho-cultural orientation affect the inter-personal relationships in the two societies.

For an Indian, his family and its direct and wider social network—the caste and the sub-caste—are virtually the beginning and the end of his human universe. He can find in the kinship group all that is meaningful in his relationships, his sociability, his security and his status. He will attribute his success to what his parents did for him, and repay his debts to them by honouring them and sharing all that his success brings. He (and his wife) will, in due course, be the recipient of similar benefits from his sons. The cardinal measure of his worth as a human being is to be found in what he is affiliated to by birth. The outstanding characteristic of Indian society, which is primarily held together by social networks, is the centripetal outlook fostered among its members. This interdependence encourages the spirit of helping one another in crisis situations like old age, even at the cost of personal necessities and comforts.

For the American, his family is strictly a sort of nursery to prepare him for a future on his own. By express definition, the family consists of a man, his wife whom he finds himself, and his minor, or in some cases, unmarried children. His parents have no permanent hold on him. Even more tenuous are his relationship with his remote relatives. His life aspirations are individual advancement and achievements, preferably as a completely free agent. He dislikes and resents being dependent on any one.

The outlook of an American is linked to his individual centred orientation and reinforced in each generation by a kinship organization dominated by the husband-wife relationship, compelling him to satisfy his social needs outside the family. Although trained to be independent, he has to depend upon other fellow human beings not only for nourishment and support but also for their faith in him, and even for trivial conversation. This poses some basic problems which he tries to solve by developing elaborate usages, rules and regulations governing interpersonal relations of all kinds. These usages, rules and regulations are designed for two purposes. On the one hand, they must guarantee his individual privacy, his right to associate with fellow human beings and to terminate such association in his best interest On the other, he has to advance them or at least maintain them. Neither of these end is always attainable to the complete satisfaction of all concerned, for the best interest of one individual does not, as a rule, accord with that of others. Furthermore, as often as not, the individual objects to the bondage of prevailing customs, practices or standards of morality and attempts to break away from them. It is this process of eternal conflict which makes American society so dynamic and exuberant. This also necessitates a number of institutionalized programmes to meet crisis situations.

The ideological foundation, the theological sinew, the thousand and one organizational details of society, and the consciously repeated educational, economic and political slogans in America—all point to the horizontal emphasis on equality and freedom. Such inequality and lack of freedom, as exist at present, are nothing but temporary imperfections to be swept away in time. And there is no doubt that the political, religious, economic and even social forces shaping society as a whole are moving, in spite of many signs to the contrary, in the direction of more freedom and greater equality for the less privileged. However, the result of the dominant egalitarian approach is often, inevitably and unsuspectedly, hierarchic when the individual is propelled by his centrifugality out of his primary group, and has to seek some other group in its place. Where his affiliation with a non-kinship group is loose because of equality and freedom, he must resort to more groups, bigger groups or better groups to ensure his desired share of sociability, security and status. The inevitable consequences are a perpetual competition among individuals into new groupings for the same purposes.

The basic difference between the two orientations is that in India the centripetal tendency is channeled within the same ideological framework so that no matter into how many castes or groups the people are divided, the desired end-results are similar and accommodating, whereas, the centrifugal American tendency makes for diversity of free associations of clubs with a variety of toally different objectives, which may have no reference to each other or may be mutually destructive. Social networks in Indian situations provide vitality to social work in properly used and strengthened to solve many problems faced by the aged rather than advocating the development of institutionalized programmes.

Social workers engaged in dealing with the problems of the aged must make a good study of the social networks in the Indian social structure. The support system available through it, in the absence of any other agency, will provide the much—needed anchor and an effective alternative to deal with the problems of such people. There is considerable difference between the individual Indian and his counterpart in Western society. We can safely say that the atomized individual found in the West is absent in India. All the studies in modernization or Westernization indicate that the process of atomization of the individual in India has hardly begun. It has not made much head-way because of the powerful hold of old traditions, as well as because of prevailing social customs, and mores and it is unlikely to proceed very far.

As a matter of fact, an Indian is never free from the web of social relations. He is ever embedded in the network of family and kinship groups, caste and locality alliances, neighbourhood ties, friendships, economic network or political groupings. He is like a spider perpetually caught in the web that feeds him and that which he too is perpetually re-creating. The process of the formation of social networks and their relationships should help us in the study, diagnosis and treatment of the problems faced by the aged in India. The relationship of social networks to society, and the influence of social environment on the client system and values, have had a rather imperfect recognition in our theoretical understanding and, therefore, have less impact on practice. It is the family and social networks which mould individuals and all aspects of life—social, economic, religious and political. It is evident that social work requires a deep understanding of social networks to maximizc its strength and minimize its strains, and to prevent welfare services from being de-humanised. Institutionalisation is not the answer to the problems of the aging in India.

Role of Elderly

Elderly through creative use of leisure, through constructive leisure time activities, can serve the community they live. These are so far untapped, massive resources in a developing country (Verma, 1981,1982,1983). The older elderly can help their younger ones in preparing for retirement from active and strenuous activities (service, business etc). However, some non-governmental organizations life Red Cross, Helpage, Clubs, religious groups and individuals are making rich contributions in this area. The elderly groups need to do it in a better, organized way and more and more elderly need to join in further enriching the quality of community life.

Hospital based, as well as community based, health services need these helps, where the illiterate rural masses of India may be lost when they first come for help. Government offices and courts are other such places where a helping and guiding hand of the elderly is necessary. Adult education and community programmes like family planning, banking loan facilities for agriculture, Medicare, child and maternal health care etc., are other areas in which the elderly can contribute. Guidance and counseling services can be made possible where education about common diseases, sex-education, marital counselling, counselling for alcohol and drug addicts etc. can be other areas of their activities. Lectures, camps, seminars etc. can be arranged for the rural and urban population regarding health and health care. Some persons have abnormal fears about ageing and relating to elderly – these need to be removed in a helpful and therapeutic atmosphere. Older elderly / senior citizens can come forward in this area of gerontophobia. More studies in this area re needed, which is described as auto gerontology (study of the aged by the aged for the aged) and all should strive to contribute. Besides, the help by the aged need not be limited to elderly only (Verma, 1996-97).

The Health Myth

The myth about health adds anxiety to the way older persons view themselves and the years they have left. Every society usually takes it for granted that the aged persons suffer from some illness or the other and that there is nothing unusual about it. It is surprising that society considers old age as synonymous with sickness. (Shanas, 1968)

Lack of Medical Aid and Poor Diet

In general, the aged people are more susceptible to illness, specifically from chronic conditions. As many of the ailments, as mentioned earlier, are common among the aged, important to discuss are the various aspects of medical care, like type of medical services preferred or availed in old age, frequency of medical care. Much relevant to this aspect of medical care are the observations of Ernest Burgers (1960) "much of the disability and ill-health of old people is the result of medical negligence. Now that the mathematical chance of surviving to old age has increased, a more positive approach to the incurable diseases of this period of life is needed to avert the personal frustration s and community problems that accompany physical disability and mental ill-health. The medical profession is beginning to realise that old people do respond to treatment and can recover to function to a surprising degree".

The socio-emotional psychological adaptation, economic or attitudinal adjustment and health and social welfare problems of the aged are so interrelated that it is difficult to separate one from the other. But the role of active aging within the "Activity" perspective has to recognize the health and medical care problems of the aged persons. To keep oneself active in some activity which may be productive in terms of economic return or unproductive for the sake of deriving pleasure or satisfaction in the leisure time available with the old, it is necessary that the old persons are educated about the preventive and promotional aspects of health so as to maintain themselves as health. In addition, medical care services have to be made accessible to them so that they be cured of the diseases or physical hazards or infirmities. In the case of an older person, it is not that much the certification of the physician based on certain signs and symptoms that would declare a person sick or ill but his subjective assessment of a health problem that would influence him to seek medical care or to utilize the available health services. Because of inherent stratification system based on different dimensions including sex and age, in the social structure of developing countries, the distribution of health and medical care services, managed mostly by government is largely uneven. Due to elite structure of health care in the developing countries, there is a skewed distribution and despite the well-taken welfare measures by the government-State, the older persons especially the women are often neglected.

Health is now being viewed more as a holistic concept because of the limitation of the functionalist perspective to consider illness or sickness within the monolithic and homogeneous social structure whose participants act under the influence of exterior defined values. Even the Interactionists, who advocate cultural pluralism as relevant to the understanding of the phenomenon of illness, seem to fall into the trap of functionalists, as their plural groups are also subservient of their values. That is why, Dingwall (1976) advocates ethno-medicine approach in understanding the concepts of health and illness as these are based on the knowledge that members of some collectivity draw on to make sense in their social and natural world and on the content and organization of that knowledge. This pluralistic approach in health care rather than functionalist monolithic model, provides a wider perspective in conceiving health and illness by including within its purview the fold and indigenous medicinal practices followed by lay persons from different socio-economic strata. Older persons, because of scarce resources at their disposal are likely to follow some of the home medications or folk health practices either to keep themselves healthy or to get cured of minor ailments. This may even include light physical or Yoga exercises which do not involve any cost and are suitable to "culture of poverty" groups.

What are the major health hazards or problems faced by older persons? No doubt, there may be many health problems more attributable to the inevitable process of aging, yet quite a few of them is due to neglect and lack of care. A study carried out in Chandigarh and the surrounding villages has revealed that the most frequently mentioned health problems by the aged are defective eyesight, general weakness, pain in joints, chronic cough and cold, defective hearing, blood pressure, digestive complaints, breathing trouble, trembling of limbs etc. (D' Souza, 1984). However, there are variations reported on sex, class and environment basis. The nature of health problems reported would need both preventive and curative care to be provided to the aging persons.

Health and medical care services: in taking productive or non-productive pursuits because of economic necessity or otherwise, one has to take care of health and medical problems of the aged. It is generally, suggested that a three-pronged approach should be followed in providing health care to the people. First, the community area and target group vulnerable to health and medical problems should be flooded with health care services so that there is adequacy of opportunity with sick persons to avail of such services. But in view of scarce resources at our disposal, we cannot provide liberal medical care to the old and aged persons in our society.

Secondly, we should provide legal protection to the needy and deserving persons. This legal approach becomes more significant in the case of the aged, who because of their limitation of physical mobility and financial constraints, are often neglected while seeking medical care at the hospital or dispensaries. There is a need to provide health insurance schems for this group and to open special window counters or provide exclusive beds in the hospitals for them. Even there should be incentive schemes for indigenous medicine practitioners including Ayurvaid and Homeopath to provide subsidized health-care to the old in the community. Though this may appear to encourage dependency of the old on the state government, yet to keep the old in fit condition for active aging , it is important. Through legislations, the elected representatives to State Assemblies and Parliament should play an active role in safeguarding the health interests of the aged persons.

Simultaneously to the above approaches, health education of the aged constitutes another important aspect of the healthcare needed so that they could learn certain do's and don'ts related to the different diseases and inculcate these in their behavioural patterns through constant practice so as to prevent the occurrence of diseases or reducing the effects of illnesses. Experience has shown that education by itself in the developing countries may not be that effective. As much, it is necessary to support it with curative services to be provided by different health personnel and agencies.

Group talks on health matters supplemented with projected media may be effective for educating this target group of the aged persons. Social gerontology should also form a part of the syllabi for medical professionals and para-professionals so that they could integrate health education along with health care to be provided to the aged persons.

Perhaps, a judicious mix of curative services, legal-protective measures and health education can become a basis for tackling the heath and medical care problems of the aged. But more than that the community members have also to be sensitized about the problems of the aged so that a greater commitment and involvement of the community leaders could be ensured in order to include "care for the aged" within the purview of Primary Health Care rather than making it a responsibility of Secondary and Tertiary Hospital Based Care.

Health Services: Availability and Access - AGED

Health service availability is defined as the presence of a service within a specific geographic area or defined population. In rural India, Primary Health Centres and Sub Centres are catering to the health needs of the people, However, they neither have geriatric wards nor specialists. Apart from these, government Hospitals at district headquarters, with moderate infrastructure and specialized medical professional cater for the health services. Depending on severity of the health problem rural people visit these hospitals. Here also no separate ward is provided for the services of the elderly.

The issue of access extends beyond the existence of a particular service to actual usage patterns relating to actual usage patterns relate to the service. Factors that influence access to service are numerous. They include geographic distance and topography, financial availability to purchase / avail the service, knowledge of services, eligibility constraints and willingness to utilize existing services. As many of the ailments, as mentioned earlier, are common among the aged, the type of medical services available, and availed by the elderly and frequency of medical care are discussed in this section .

In one of his study related to medical care and elderly, Burgess (1960) described that "much of the disability and ill health of old people is the result of medical negligence. Now that the mathematical chance of surviving to old age has increased, a more positive approach to the incurable diseases of this period of life is needed to avert the personal frustrations and community problems that accompany physical disability and mental ill-health. The medical profession is beginning to realize that old people do respond to treatment and can recover to function to a surprising degree".

Nutrition and Ageing - AGED

Diet, nutrition and ageing has been a fertile field for research without any clear-cut information about the nature of linkage. The only one fact which has stood the test of time is that calorie restriction prolongs life span of experimental animals. The common implication from that fact is the obese elderly will die much earlier than normal or even a lean individual. Though several epidemiological evidences of indirect nature exist, the area of nutrition and ageing is still unexplored.

There are other areas in nutrition which are yet to be explored in ageing. Of special interest is the role of several micro-nutrients like vitamin A Beta – carotene, vitamins C and E and Selenium which are powerful anti-oxidants in the human body. Numerous trials with human subjects have been and are being undertaken to as certain the role of anti-oxidants in either preventing or controlling the free-radical damages in blood vessels which might lead to coronary and cerebral disorders. There are research studies in the western world which in dictate that the anti-oxidants can also play part in delaying the process of ageing. Development of dietary guideline for elderly individuals is an area of urgency in India. There are a number of studies which indicate that path-physiological changes in taste buds leads to altered food preferences. At the same time, reduction in digestive enzymes and alteration of gastro-intestinal motility need a dietary pattern different from the one practiced in earlier years. This is an area which is of considerable importance for the elderly themselves, their careers and those who are in charge of old-age homes.

Government of India is giving much priority to health programs to bring 'health for all by 2000 A.D.' Perhaps so far whatever measures taken towards amelioration the health problems of the aged, are purely 'ad hoc' in character. This issue cannot be left for the future and needs immediate attention of the policy makers and administrators. Like children the aged too need health and personal care and hence there is need to establish separate geriatric wards in the hospitals with geriatric professional. It is also suggested to implement mobile geriatric care centres which will cover more number of the elderly in rural areas. In rural areas majority of the families are not in a position to bear the cost of long term care of the elderly and hence, government can think about subsidized medical care for elderly. Implementing the health insurance scheme in rural areas will be a helpful security to the elders. Voluntary Organisations should also be encouraged to play a meaningful role in this regard.

Health care is important, but at the same time one should not forget the importance of social care and informal helping relationship within the family and community that maintain integrity and well being. Gerontologists have documented the crucial role that these non-formal, natural support systems play in providing social care and their enormous role in the lives of the elderly (Cantor, 1980). Demographic projections are warning the possible increase of growing population in India in the coming years. Keeping this in mind, it is time now to think seriously how to provide the health security to the rural elderly and suitable steps have to be taken to improve the quality of life of elderly of today and tomorrow.

Optimal Diet

Effective disease prevention is a combination of nutrition, physical activity, mental health and medical care. Nutrition deserves considerable attention in the practice of preventive geriatrics to achieve goal of health ageing.

The basic approaches of dietary assessment, counseling and supplementation can reduce the likelihood of nutrient inadequacies and provide primary protection. Disease prevention through dietary management is a cost effective approach to promote healthy ageing. Many common chronic conditions of ageing can be prevented or at least attenuated by prudent nutritional intervention. Fats, cholesterol, soluble fibres and trace elements like copper and chromium are known to affect the morbidity and mortality due to is chaemic heart disease. Again, a reduced sodium intake and increasing potassium intake are known to improve the control of hypertension. The antioxidant vitamin A and beta carotene vitamin C, vitamin E and trace mineral like selenium may protect against various types of cancer. A decrease in simple carbohydrate and an increase in soluble dietary fiber may normalize moderately elevated blood glucose levels. deficiencies of zinc and iron diminish immune function. adequate levels of calcium and vitamin D can help to prevent senile osteoporosis.

Dietary measures can be applied to all levels of prevention. Primary prevention aims to prevent a disease or condition in a healthy, asymptomatic individual. Although dietary recommendations do exist for specific diseases and conditions, a more general dietary pattern with sufficient variety can protect individuals against a wide spectrum of diseases. With regard to secondary prevention, correction of inadequate calcium intake in a patient at risk for osteoporosis, reduction of elevated serum cholesterol in a patient at risk for coronary heart disease, or identification of risk for poor nutritional status in general with subsequent intervention are some of the examples. Tertiary prevention by dietary measures is also feasible, e.g., dietary management of elevated serum lipids in a diabetic patient or dietary management of blood pressure in hyper-tensive patients.

Balanced Diet for elderly: The diet of elderly needs some modification due to lower physical activity in them and consequent 10-11% less energy required by them. Diet should be cheap, balanced and property based on recommended dietary allowances. Some of the simple tips include liberal intake of green vegetables, fluids, semisolids and frequent but small meals. Avoid fried foods and fasting and reduce total fat, refined carbohydrate and salt intake. The diet should be easy to cook and the one that can be stored. Ready to eat recipes should be known to individuals. Table V gives the balanced diet for an elderly persons for a day with regard to quantities of food intake and approximate nutrients supplied.

Table V

Balanced Diet for an Elderly Persons for a Day

Foodstuffs	*Quantify raw gms.*	
	Males	*Females*
Cereals	350	225
Pulses	50	40
Vegetables	200	150
Green leafy vegetables	50	50
Roots and Tubers	100	100
Fruits	200	200
Milk and Milk Products	300	300
Sugar	20	20
Fats and Oils	25	20

Approximate Nutrients Supplied

Foodstuffs	*Quantify raw gms.*	
	Males	*Females*
Calories	2200	1700
Protein	65 g.	50 g.
Fat	50 g.	40 g.
Calcium	1 g.	0.9 g.
Iron	38 mg.	30 mg.
Vitamin A (Rational)	1030 mg.	930 mg.
Thiamine	1.96 mg	1.45 mg.
Riboflavin	1.78 mg	1.51 mg.

Myths about Aged Persons

The Social myth

The Social myths are defined sociologically as false social beliefs about social groups. The basic problem of a social myth is its potential to make its victims act so that the myth becomes a self fulfilling prophecy. Specially, if older persons accept the common belief that they lose the capacity to function well, they themselves may come to believe what others think and say about them, and they begin to function below their actual capacity. Information presented below could be relevant for understanding these

Social Myths

Majority of the elderly (53.3%) were fond to be not heading their families and among them most of the elderly (108/160)

were found to be widowed. In-most of the families, sons of the elderly consider that aged persons do not have the capacity to head families and that particularly aged widowers lose more capacity to function well. On the other hand, aged persons themselves may come to falsely believe that due to old age they lost all the capacities for heading the family. The chi-square test result shows a highly significant association between marital status and leadership in families. The data also demonstrates that despite old age, 140 (46.78%) elderly could head the family.

Table : Heading the Family

Marital Status	*Heading the family*	*Not heading the family*	*Total*
Never married	57.1(4)	42.9(3)	2.3(7)
Currently married	63.7(86)	36.3(49)	45.0(135)
Widowed	30.8(48)	69.2(108)	52.0(156)
Divorced/ Separated	100.0(2)	-	0.7(2)
Total	46.7(140)	53.3(160)	100.0(300)

$X^2 = 34.17910$; df = 3; p=0.0000. (Percentages among categories are row-wise and among totals are table-wise.)

1. Healthy ageing alone leads active ageing; health of the older people depends on the prevailing economic, political, social, cultural, educational and physical environment. This multi-dimensional supportive environment needs to be planned and developed by the individual, family, community, and institutions, NGOs, Governments and International Organisations for the welfare and care of the aged.

2. Promotion of health is the most important part of the total health care of the aged. To maintain and promote

health during old age, it is vital to prevent diseases and disability. Early detection and appropriate care should follow when preventive measures taken up, 50 percent or more of all the health problems are preventable. Positive attitude towards life coupled with exercise and good nutrition makes a big difference in your over all quality.

1. Ageing process varies from community to community depending upon factors like-ethnic and culture, climatic conditions, geographic location, family size, gender, genetic background, disease experience in life, nutrition, infections, life style and education. Those who formulate ageing programmes should consider these factors in developing the activities.

2. Ageing starts from the day of conception and therefore, the active ageing activities should be initiated early in life and not when people are sixty plus. In India, unfortunately, women have lower life span than men. This is mainly due to inappropriate treatment given to female foetus, girl child and women during the reproductive phase. All these factors should be considered in formulating active ageing programmes for women in addition to what is done for the men.

3. If the older people are enabled and encouraged, they can be a valuable asset to the family and to the community. They are not an economic and social burden to the family and the community. Old age is prone to develop chronic diseases like diabetes, Cardio-vascular problems, cancer, mental disorders, arthritis and disability of vision and hearing etc. Appropriate care need to be provided to older persons to meet these conditions effectively, older people could be both receivers and providers of care.

4. With increasing urbanization and individualism, more and more nuclear families are coming up. This is bound to have adverse affect on the life of the aged. Family system which was supportive of old people is fast disappearing, requires readjustment in life situation and inter-personal relationships. This readjustment can improve the psycho-social well being of the aged.

5. The elderly keeping normal health to reasonable extent should conceive and develop an activity to spend their time productively by using their wisdom and experience to the extent possible which enables them to age actively.

6. Active ageing requires a firm foundation of good health derived from healthy life styles since childhood. Apart from caring for physical health, participation in activities with in and out side the household contributes to the optimal approach and attitude towards active ageing.

7. To facilitate participation of older persons in the economic life of the society by creating conditions conductive to employment. The right of older persons to employment should be based on ability to perform the work rather than the chronological age.

8. Organisational frame work and programmes at central and state level should be accepted for implementation including setting up of:
   (i) National Board of senior citizens.
   (ii) National Institute for senior citizens.

   Formulations of policies and special programmes for schemes such as construction of homes for the elderly, maintenance of the destitute elderly in homes, day-care centres to improve the quality of life as elderly, foster care services for them etc; and constitute a committee for welfare of senior citizens at the state level.

11. The financial and other social support should be provided through Government and Non-government organizations especially to the Lower income groups to maintain their elders.

12. The aged should be encouraged to form their voluntary organizations and cooperatives, which should be helped by the Government under their programmes as grant-in-aid for undertaking social services.

13. Certain measures like preferential allocation of land for group Housing Societies for the elderly. House building advances need to be integrated in the National Housing Policy.

14. Senior citizens should be asked to serve the public cause in their individual capacities. They may provide on the spot assistance to victims of crime and accidents and provide useful information for crime detection and prevention. Services of the senior citizens in villages should be linked with rural development of the remote areas.

15. Further, necessary infra structural facilities of transport, health and other services, travel concession by all modes of transport, recreational activities and day-care centres to interact with persons with commonality of interests and discuss common problems which may lead to alleviation of emotional problems of the elderly.

16. To cope with emergent medical and psychological problems greater emphasis needs to be given on geriatric

medicine both in teaching and practice for geriatric asse4ssment.

17. Facilities on education and training should be available for doctors, para-medical personnel and social workers from voluntary and governmental circles to impart training in geriatrics and gerontology covering all aspects of old age ailments. Families should also be oriented on health and nutrition needs of the elderly and ways to meet them through specially brought out literature, book lets and mass-media.

4

Coping With Old Age

Old age poses a particular momentum in one's life when not only physical sensory-motor conditions decline, but more specially, one is confronted with multiple social and psychological challenges, such as the loss of friends frequent marginalisation from work positions, the fear of imminent diseases and impairment, the approach of death and so on. Questions as to the possibility of a healthy and enjoyable old age often involve disputable interchanges among different areas, like biological models of human ageing tend to emphasise the decline of human capacities, where as psychological models tend to consider that human capacities can open to learning and adaptation even when sensory-motor adjustments perish (Labouvie-Vief, 1982). To become old involves facing challenges. Recent works on old age has pointed out the psychological demands that have to be met in having to adjust oneself to different and difficult conditions of living. (Messy, 1992; Veyset. 1989). Nevertheless, not all the individuals re prepared to deal with such demands adequately. Thus, the question is what makes some old people abler than others face the challenges of the ageing process? What sort of "Competence" is useful as one gets old? What are the chances, and then one could ask, of an enjoyable and fulfilling old age?

In their paper "Coping in old Age", Lucia Rabello Decastro and G. Rabello Decastro (2001) have proposed to understand coping mechanisms at old age are held to be the result of a life long process which enables old people to better adjust themselves to the multiple challenges of ageing process. Two case studies in the form of life histories are presented and analysed in 9order to illustrate how through out one's lifetime inner resources and potentialities can be restrained or expanded. Further, it is argued that cultural dispositions can egitimate a view of the self as multiple so that individual can fare better in managing the challenges the old age thwarts.

Coping mechanisms is thus fundamental at advanced stage when diverse and multiple challenges affect human lives. To grow old means to face and cope up with the threat of helplessness, dependency and loneliness (Hess, 1987). Perhaps, it is one of the most challenging moments of human existence, which supports the idea of an enjoyable and satisfactory old age results from life long process of dealing with hardships, which may be regarded as opportunities for expanding inner resources.

Healthy Ageing

Healthy ageing dwells on the fact that though ageing is a natural, inevitable and inexorable phenomenon, one can find better way to live it positively and actively. The term "Healthy Ageing" is often used to emphasise that ageing is not a disease. In other words ageing period should be as healthy as possible and reasonably meaningful confirming to the WHO slogan. "It is not sufficient to add years to life but the more important objective is to add life to years". In India and other countries, aged people are described as old and senile. In recent years several positive terms are being used to describe them as senior citizen, elderly, third age individuals and individuals in the twilight of their life. Who are aged individuals? All individuals of 60+ are elderly. This is the cut off point prescribed by the

United Nations. Recent studies conducted in physiology, bio-chemistry and epidimiology have confirmed that all aged individuals cannot be put in one homogeneous group. They can be categorized in to "young-old", between the age of 60 to 7 5 years, "old-old" between 75 to 85 years and "very old" between 86 years and above. The first stage categories are physically active and mentally alert, and in most cases they are not dependent on others while the second and third categories need support and help. Numerous scientific studies have confirmed that the life span of Homo-Sapiens is possibly around 120 years. With better health care and better standard of living there is no reason why man will not cross hundred years and more. Throughout the world, attention is now being focused on the elderly of tomorrow and in which the health promoting behaviour for ensuring healthy ageing should be initiated.

Elderly and Community Mental Health

The question then arises whether those elderly can contribute to the community and country at large? S.K. Verma and Ashima Nehra (2001) in their article "Elderly and community Mental Health" feel that the growing population of elderly (both young elderly and old elderly) every where but particularly in a developing country life India has to be seen as a boon in disguise. They are not only the consumers of mental health services of the country but can be real producers of community mental health services, and must be seen in that light, particularly in view of the limited resources in trained man-power. Their vast experiences over the years need to be harnessed in the years to come, if the dream of "Health for All" by the year 2000 A.D. may be achieved. Why let go waste such a huge reservoir of experiences in various fields just because of our own faulty attitudes towards them and their problems? It we do not utilize such an available rich resource, then who is to blame? And why cry over limited resources? It is high time to over come these draw backs and sooner it is done the better it would be better for the community.

Community mental health appears as an abstraction. It can be seen through various manifestations indicating positive mental health of the community. The positive indications are level of co-operation among its various individuals, families, groups, units, institutions as manifested in sharing experiences, happiness, even grief, in sharing community achievements, healthy interpersonal relations, medical facilities, law and order as well as in absence of negative indicators like wars, conflicts, social discrimination on the basis of caste, religion, sex, etc. (ICMR Report, 1997). These constitute what is known as quality of community life (QCL) and it is here the elderly can contribute much through Governmental and non-Governmental agencies and even at one's own individual levels.

Criteria of Adjustment

Criteria of adjustment refer to standards and norms employed to assess the degree and quality of personal and social adjustment of the aged. The focus of this sociological framework to analyse their family and social adjustment may include such areas of analysis:

(i) Family adjustment

(a) Satisfaction with the sibling treatment

(b) Satisfactory relationship with wife and other family members, other than siblings in the family.

(c) Satisfaction with home life.

(ii) Social adjustment

(a) Favourable attitude towards social participation with others known/unknown.

(b) Effective relationship with Social realities and situations.

(c) Ability to get along with other persons.

(d) Successful adjustment with different groups and subgroups.

(e) Possession of socially desirable attributes. (Description of self as sociable, likeable, popular and able to get along with different kinds of people etc.)

(iii) Economic/Financial adjustment

(a) Re-employment / no employment conditions and satisfaction.

(b) Motivation in seeking re-employment.

(iv) Political/Social Work Interests

(a) Leisure time activities

(b) Religious beliefs and practices.

(c) Participation in voluntary organizations.

(v) Problems and stresses

(a) Financial / Occupational.

(b) Familial, Neighbourhood.

(c) Health problems.

(d) Insecurity, loneliness and emotional support problems.

The Future of Ageing

In a society that places a high value on youth, vitality and physical attractiveness; older people tend to become invisible. Recent years, however, have seen some changes in attitudes towards old age. Older people are unlikely to recover the full authority and prestige that used to be accorded to elders of the community in ancient societies. Yet as they have come to comprise a larger proportion of population, older people have come to comprise a larger proportion of population, older people have acquired more political influence than they used to have. They have already become a powerful political lobby.

The later years of life can be seen as a time of great opportunity and even celebration provided aged people acquire new outlook towards the life. With their positive mental outlook and good physical shape of body these individuals can continue to grow learn and explore. Travelling, pursuing further education on developing new skills, doing small jobs in family, helping grand children with their education and their by keeping themselvės well occupied and busy. A few suggestions for personal growing and healthy well being of the aged may be outlined as:

(i) Face new opportunities, challenges and experiments
(ii) Adopt to the uses of new technology
(iii) Maintain creativity in its new forms
(iv) Seek avenues for volunteerism and intergenerational activities
(v) Maintain social contacts and
(vi) Continue with spiritual activities through various media.

Thus to conclude information revolution that brings about basic changes even if they occur over a relatively long period of time necessitate the need for a successful restructuring of the ageing process. To face these new challenges and to adapt to the uses of new technology, one needs to get involved in active learning and creativity in a new form, which also requires mechanisms to seek avenues for volunteerism and intergenerational activities..

1. Use of Indigenous and Innovative Ideas

Introducing mobility in the care system gives considerable support to the families having the aged living with them. Mobile Hospital Vans can cover the entire locality and provide treatment for minor ailments to the young and old on nominal charges. This service is specially useful for the middle aged caregivers who are caught between demands of children on the one side and ailing elderly people on the other. Further, instead of expensive allopathic treatment, less expensive homeopathic or Ayurvedic medicines can be tried. In all these cases training the staff to handle the aged and motivating community health care workers to work with them and their families is a necessary requirement.

Since the number of seniors among the poorer sections is on the increase and in view of the socio-economic situation of the country. Much more support will have to be provided to the poor families. Organising the least expensive programmes which can meet, at least, the basic requirements of the poor and destitute may be considered. It is worth examining whether traditional practices or indigenous ideas can be used to help the aged. For example, common halls with basic infrastructural facilities and a series of row houses like Dharmashalas or choultries can be built and let out to the needy poor. Sanatoria can also be built for the aged who can stay for a brief period to give relief to the families. Similarly facilities may be provided on a large scale in holy cities, near shrines and places or pilgrimages. The aged can stay either in groups or separately as long as they want to live there.

2. Self - Reliance – What Seniors can do for Themselves

Self-reliance and self health care of the elderly are the bases of any support programme. To be effective these should be backed up by adequate health, social, legal and family support systems. If integration of the retired generations in the community is the aim, they should be looked after by the family and every effort needs to be made to provide the able and willing elders with suitable remunerative occupations. The aging population is expensive if not used effectively. Their service must be utilized for the good of both the retired persons and others.

Long years of settled work-life instills a habit routine with fixed expectations and few changes. Retirement disrupts this. Post-retirement life involves several sharp changes in status, roles and life style demanding adaptation. Further, many reach their pinnacles of position on the verge of retirement. Many develop effective bonds with their jobs and its paraphernalia which lead to serve emotional stress on their loss. These changes are often traumatic, to reduce this trauma, one needs to develop a certain behavioural flexibility by getting used to deprivations that may characterize retirement. The transitions from middle age to old age or retirement is similarly fraught with changes in roles and responsibilities. A sense of identity is indispensable to all individuals. Senior citizens organizations all over stand evidence to the elders need for identity. In retirement, one has to relate oneself meaningfully to others and this is best done by participation in peer group activities. There could be many things to share mutually among peers than with those of other generations. Such activities and social exchanges with peers is mutually rewarding experience. It should also compensate the losses of work oriented social contacts due to retirement. Senior citizens must make every effort to be self-reliant, cooperate with one another and make efforts to develop mentally and spiritually to avoid loneliness. Boredom and suffering.

To maintain physical and mental health and to lead an active life for several years, the elderly must work for it. An idle life or retirement leads to clogging of the body and sluggishness of the mind. They must be conscious of the importance of the sense organs and the need for their care until something goes wrong. The aged should, in the first instance, convince themselves that they should be fully concerned about their health, take preventive care and adapt their life-style to their health status. They should not believe in the statement that old age is synonymous with dependency and ill-health, or that age deprives the person of much of his mental capacity and productive abilities. The aged must learn to put up with minor irritants in the family and participate in the household work. They should develop a more tolerant attitude, and appreciate the difficulties faced by the younger members of the family. Meet the like minded elderly persons, form groups, develop common hobbies and find out the organizations which can utilize their services. There are innumerable activities like guiding the unemployed, help disabled, engaging in environmental protection activities, spreading literacy, making people community health conscious, reading for the blind, playing with slum children, helping the family members in house-hold chores and many more. The government can take a number of steps to help the aged by helping their families. For example, persons taking care of the aged should be entitled to rebate in income tax... Free insurance cover should be provided to senior citizens against accidents and for health care. In addition to providing grants, the government can allot suitable plots of land free of cost for starting geriatric clinics, old age homes, and senior citizens' centres. Senior officers in government or those who have retired from high positions can also be helpful in securing grants-in-aid. In short, to launch an effective programme of helping the seniors, the family, the community and the government must work in a coordinated manner with the active participation of seniors. In fact, it is to seniors who should take lead in tackling their present and future problems. Senior citizens must make every effort to be self-reliant, cooperate with one another and set a good example to the rest of the community.

In India where familial bondages exist and probably will continue for a long time, relating oneself meaningfully to the family and to children is a useful experience. Participation in the home making functions in supportive familial roles could be highly satisfying provided one exercises enough caution not to intrude or interfere into what the children consider their legitimate domains or spheres of authority and action. A major factor contributing to the happiness in old age is economic independence. The elderly must try and supplement family income when it is possible. Children do not feel their parents as burdensome as long as they maintain normal life. They also expect the aged to learn to put up with day-to-day inconveniences due to living conditions especially in urban areas.

The elderly have some special abilities. Many are endowed with detachment and perspective, they can analyse the contemporary socio-economic and political events with serene detachment, moderate the extremists unthinking enthusiasm, and monitor the doings of the unscrupulous politician. They can educate the young, not by preaching to them, but by setting an example and by sharing their joys and sorrows with them. Thus the wisdom and experience of the old could be combined with the energy and enthusiasm of the young to build a new world order, where all the members of the human family can live in wholesome harmony. The elders can take initiative in forming mixed groups, where young and old, rich and poor, men and women, can form coalitions of power and shared humanity. Age indeed is a universalizing factor, transcending petty considerations of caste, creed, race, colour and sex. This mixed group will fuse the energy and enthusiasm of the young with the caution and mellowness of the old, thus bringing out the best in both.

3. Developing Inner Strength

All classes have recourse to spiritual activities in their old age. The upper classes have got many more ways of spending their free time, while many aged persons belonging to weaker sections have recourse to religious practices not merely in order to find solace from loneliness, but even to make use of their spare time, since they cannot afford any other diversion. These activities help the people to turn within and develop their inner strength.

Indian philosophy teaches that employment is a duty and only a means to livelihood and not livelihood itself. Excessive ego involvement in work develops a strong emotional cathexis or "Bandha" which one might find very difficult to outgrow.

Therefore, a gradual withdrawal of emotional investment while retaining the cognitive involvement is envisaged during the penultimate stage of life, the Vanaprasthasrama. One could play the roles appropriately, actively participate in the discharge of social responsibilities and activities but with reduced emotional entanglement. In simple language work is for work's sake, or to help others and not so much for self aggrandizement. The imbibing of such a philosophy of life is beautifully depicted in the Mahabharata and the Bhagavad Gita. It contains the traditional Indian approach for a happy retirement. Those who conform to this Indian view of life in the older years experience less trauma and fewer problems than those who do not subscribe to an unquestioned faith in God as an omnipotent force ruling over the destinies of man. It seems to offer succour to a troubled mind in the face of disease, disability and disaster. After all, one has to have the serenity to accept things one cannot change.

The spriritual values and ideals that are inherent in the Indian notion of stages of life cycle may not be practical alternatives given the contemporary situation. But the basic idea behind it is important. It reflects an acknowledgement that ageing may cause psychological strain as well as economic burden to society. Enjoining certain duties and attitude to the stages of Vanaprastha and Sanyas represent a kind of ancient solution to the problems involved in ageing. Apart from the Spiritual Ideals behind it, it seeks to ensure that the elderly may not cause unnecessary economic burden to the family and society, and at the same time could enjoy the status and respect and a state of harmonious psychological existence in the even-changing society.

Developing sense of detachment and working for a desired goal without expecting any results which is known as desireless action takes a long way in maintaining the much needed tranquility. Its importance and relevance in old age are obvious.

In Search of Better Living for the Aged

The aging of population is a process whereby the proportions of children in the population decrease and the proportions of old persons increase. Aging and longevity of life are relatively new phenomena experienced by the developed countries. Due to scientific and technological progress and consequent success of health care measures, the reduction in fertility rate, a relative rise in the economic level and contact with the developed world, the demographic pattern in developing countries is undergoing change. It has already lead to significant increase in life expectancy, and in the proportion and absolute number of the elderly population. This potential for aging exerts influence not only on economic, but also on the family, the community and the state-the three major supporting institutions.

Although families continue to remain strong and exert major influences on the behaviour of individuals and groups, the effectiveness of family as the most important institution in delivering care is fast reducing, particularly in urban areas where the traditional extended family is slowly disintegrating. The increasing participation of women in the work and preference of young people for nuclear family have further reduced the availability of family support. The gradual breakdown of the extended family system has been creating negative psychological effects such as alienation, loneliness and other emotional stress.

What we may be facing is the disintegration of the family as an effective, spontaneous and rich support system and its replacement by a weaker substitute. With the population getting older, the leading support role of the family acquires added significance, even more so because the aged population itself is getting older. With radical changes in family composition and interrelation among members, sharing of problems of ageing with the family and community is difficult. Thus, for elderly, the problems of ageing are increasingly to become an individual affair. Previously family and public sharing helped to defuse the "Private terror" which posed problems to the individual. The psychological consequence of this for the old are obvious.

Apprehension about Becoming Old

Most human beings are awfully afraid of becoming old. This is not only due to the fear of declining health in old age but also due to the fact that most human societies place a premium on young age and seem to ignore the old. The youth dominated societies of today do not seem to care for those who had been occupying high positions and performing significant roles a few years earlier. That is why most of us are apprehensive about becoming old and quite a few of us would prefer an early death rather than suffering the innumerable problems at every stage of life. But it is conceivable that the problems required to be faced in old age may be more difficult and of a different nature to the problems of young or middle age. Moreover, human beings are less prepared, both physically and mentally, to face problems in old age. As such, the problems faced by the elderly of society merit special attention by sociologists and psychologists.

The beginning of old age in an individual is associated with different conditions or changes occurring in life, such as the graying of the hair, the advent of bifocals, a serious impairment of vital physical components, failure of the individual to function independently, ceasing to be productive and imposition of an arbitrary retirement age by society. Old age means physical disability; declining mental ability, the gradual giving up of roles-playing in social activities, and a shift in economic status, moving from economic independence to economic dependence on others for support (Soodan, 1975: 112).

The roles played by the old in the family in the joint family system of the pre-industrial society has lost much of its significance due to the emergence of the nuclear family system. The old are not properly cared for by their children. The present industrial society is not beneficial for the old people who do not get satisfaction of their physical, social and psychological needs. Aging has become a complex challenging proposition for the individual. As Bengston and Orbach have stated due to the absence of norms and lack of socialization facilities for the old people, they do not find any guidelines for their actions and thereby experience the lost feelings. (Bengstion, 1973 : 24-31 Orbach 1973 : 53-63). As T.S. Saraswathi, Mushira Hakim and Shagufa Kapadia have stated, the best insurance of the aged, the joint family, is becoming increasingly unpopular, nuclear families being on the increase in most parts of the country. In a competitive society, where usefulness is measured by economic yardsticks, the aged are useless (T.S. Saraswathi, Mushira Hakim and Shagufa Kapadia, 1982 : 5-6). They have also stated that many factors have given rise to the aging process in India: migration of younger members to cities or abroad for employment, a rising cost of living without parallel increase in resources, especially of the older generation; earlier retirement age in some fields; corrosion of values and the emergence of the nuclear family with increasing stress on individuality (Ibid, 1982:6).

The nature of the problems of old age differs from society to society. In the case of Indian society, the situation is somewhat different than some of the western societies. In the rural communities of India, the joint family system still prevails to a large extent. The old in these communities are not thrown on the mercy of society by their families. Moreover, they are owners of property and therefore given proper attention by their family members. The older people in the agrarian communities remain financially independent. They are not only owners of the land holdings but also participate in the productive activities as much as they can, according to their health which is why the older people in the Indian rural communities still enjoy a high status and play the decision making role in the family.

The situation is slightly different in the case of the urban communities. The joint family system is not prevalent to the same extent as in the rural communities. The urbanites may be maintaining links with their joint families, but most of them live in nuclear families and so cannot avail themselves of the benefits provided by the joint family system. The problems of aging in urban India are therefore becoming somewhat similar to those prevailing in the industrialized societies of the west. However, this is only a trend and to a large extent the older people in the urban areas still enjoy a fairly high status in their families and are generally well respected by them.

India is a developing country and the number of aged people has also increase with better health and medical facilities and reduction in death rates. In India, the number of aged above 55 years was 29.97, 32.69, 44.19 and 62.84 millions in 1951, 1961, 1971 and 1981, respectively. The percentage increase of the aged has been 9.07 per cent over the decade 1951-61; 35.15 per cent over 1961-71 and 42.19 per cent over 1971-81. These figures indicate the increasing trend of aged population in India (Satyavathi and Murthy, 1976 : 11-13 and Parthasarthy, 1980 : 380-388).

According to Burgess, the problem of old age has emerged as a social one, to some extent due to the rising proportion of the aged in the population, but, to a larger extent due to the declining roles and status of old aged people in the industrial society of the present world (Burgess Ernest, 1951 : 7-8). The old used to avail of more opportunities to satisfy their obvious requirements in the pre-industrial society. They participated in the productive activities as specialists, in societies dominated by agricultural and handicraft economies. This directly or indirectly depended on their physical health and therefore they remained financially independent. There was no procedure of compulsory retirement at a set age till 1900 and people used to continue their occupational activities according to their physical fitness. Moreover, it is considered the duty of their children to provide financial, physical and other types of security to their parents in their old age. In the joint faimilies they were given the powerful position of decision makers and advisers in recognition of their knowledge and wide experience of life. The pre-industrial society clearly gave full opportunities to its old people for the fulfillment of their different requirements. Many scholars believe that in view of increased urbanization, modernization, industrialization and inflationary economic trends, the Indian society, which at one time looked after the elderly, has undergone a dramatic change and become indifferent towards the aged. The roles and status of the aged have decreased and the knowledge and experience of the old people has lost significance in the present day Indian society.

The shift from an agricultural society to an industrial society has reduced employment opportunities for the older persons (Eugene A. Fried Man, 1960 : 120-162). Yet, Clark Tibbitts finds that continuous expansion and growth of productivity through high energy technology of the present has created a situation of abundance in modern industrial society. The ability to support econoimically non-productive segments of the population has increased immensely with the growth of modern industrial technology (Clark Tibbitts, 1960 : 336). According to Talmon, the old do not achieve higher status even in the family. From the point of view of the older person, the loss of some of their former tasks such as instruction of the young or supervision of household crafts may have diminished their utility and thus weakened the bond with the younger generation (Talmon, 1961 : 284-295).

Markers of Old Age

Increasing physical and mental decline mark old age. An important identification of being old is physical appearance. People are defined as old if they look old: white hair, bifocals, wrinkled skin, bent position and so on, are changes contributing to the ageing of appearance. Old age is characterized by an objective condition of social, economic, and family marginality, by a role crisis and identity crisis. It is characterized by changes in physical and intellectual capacities. One indication of old age occurs when the individual relinquishes his occupational role. Parsons (1954:103) states, "retirement leaves the older man in a peculiarly functionless position, cut off from participation in the most important interests and activities of the society." Few incentives exist for older persons to make productive contributions to society, and obstacles to their engagement in productive activities exist. Among men, the transition from active adult status to retirement is often even more traumatic, relative poverty and deprivation accompany this retirement, elderly individuals experience an even greater loss of identity and personal worth. In old age, most people experience definite losses in efficiency or even complete inability to work. The elderly have to contend with the experience of a deep sense of alienation from non-participation. Although retirement is primarily about relinquishing paid employment yet it has generally been problematised in terms of growing old. The age of retirement thus shapes the last stage of life.

In rural areas, old age is identified as a period of life when a slide from independence to dependency on others takes place. This slide may arise due to both poor health and age. Among peasant communities, handing over of property by an ageing individual to others belonging to the younger generation symbolizes the crossing of the threshold of age, of a person.

Among women, the transition to old age occurs with menopause. The physical and psychological problems associated with menopause when coupled with the departure of children from the home can be traumatic for a woman. The effects of this, on an ageing woman's life can be profound.

Changing appearance can be extremely hard for a woman to bear who has always prided herself on her appearance; the same applies to a man who has always emphasized his physical strength which he now sees declining. Ageing of the skin is a reflection of a lifetime of physical changes, environmental exposures, and personal behaviours. The skin acts as a major indicator of visible age and is used as a "marker' to judge attractiveness and desirability. It becomes a continuous reminder of the passage of time for both men and women.

Throughout people's lives there exists a continuity of roles and a smoothness of passage from status to another. However, on reaching old age there is a sudden disruption in the continuity of socialization. While the elderly persons continue to retain the values and beliefs acquired by them in life, they do not have a clear role-set for their new status of being old. Ambiguity characterizes the roles of the old. While most people are faced with loss of some important roles, they often encounter the prospect of not knowing what to replace these roles with. Old age is often a difficult period for the individual and those close to him/her. Becoming older means negotiating social roles, relations and expectations.

Old age as a social role is characterized by chronological years, by one's stage in personality, and by societal definitions. In general, the individual's chronological age and appearance will influence his/her age role. In the family, the elderly individual is defined perhaps as a grandparent or by his loss of authority over his adult children. The process of becoming older "can involve acquiring new forms of power, influence and security, particularly in the context of the family" (Fogharty, 1975). Further, the role and status of the elderly is often evaluated with a view to their willingness and ability to aid the family financially, do household chores, or help bring up children.

From the socio-cultural perspective an individual is termed aged when he distances himself from those roles and statuses which he was performing as an adult.

He becomes disengaged from his normal adult roles such as withering away from the family roles and constricting the community of friends (Tyagi, 1996).

The declining social responsibility and role attrition of the elderly are reflected in their shrinking social world. Sociologically, they display the decrements of retirement, widowhood, declining health and income, reduced group memberships and social interaction. This involves the loss and emptying of roles, both in number and content. For women, the contraction of domestic roles begins in middle age when the first child leaves home and also when the daughter-in-law comes and is welcomed into the household, continues into old age, especially after widowhood. For men the role attrition starts about the same time with an easing of work activity and continues after retirement. Dowd (1974) indicates, "the problems of ageing are essentially problems of decreasing power resources... money, approval, esteem or respect and compliance." Even the basic material economic and health needs, are an inevitable consequence of the relationship between individual and society, their problems include a feeling of material insecurity or dependence, and attenuated intergenerational relationships. The elderly persons are also said to be gradually losing their decision-making authority. They are likely to suffer a sense of psychic dispossession that reflects loss of roles and status.

Clothes also transmit age-related messages. Lurie (1981) shows how conceptions of age-appropriate clothing confirm the association between physical ageing and decline. She notes that the tradition of marking the transition froln maturity to old age by a change of custom is well established. Certain garments such as the shawl come to be associated with old age partly because they may be worn for extra warmth. Other garments become associated with old age for reasons, which are less obvious and linked to movements of fashion.

Society may be offended, when men or women do not dress to their age. Very often, the source of offence or deviation here is not the fact being old but the refusal to accept the state.

With advancing age, a time comes when memories fade, bones snap. Growing old also implies decline in mental faculties. Old age is distinguished by a general slowing in the timing of behaviour. It adversely affects the elderly person's speed of response. Old people are reckoned to process information more slowly than the younger age groups. With increasing age, signs of decline in cognition are witnessed. Some of the commonly used terms in Indian society to denote this decline in cognitive abilities, are Smriti Brabstha (loss of memory), Sathiya Gaya (Senile, turned sixty), and Sathar Bathar Ho Gaya (turned seventy; a term used in parts of North India, particularly, Punjab).

Old age is depicted positively in terms of maturity, wisdom, compassion, and the potential for spiritual growth as well as self-acceptance. For some, attributes of wisdom and serenity are positive aspects of being older. The old person is a source of wisdom based on the rich experience longevity has made possible. He is the repository of knowledge transmitted by word of mouth from generation to generation. In the little community, the scarcity value of older persons undoubtedly contributed to the age deference patterns that characterize it. We have much to learn from these elderly, whose lives are a rich montage of traditions, experiences and beliefs. In mass society, their scarcity value is lost, and their prestige is accordingly diminished. The best things about old age include freedom to do and to be what one wishes. That is, freedom from responsibility and freedom from worry about others opinions. The elderly try to maintain positive self-concepts by narrowing their social worlds to avoid exposure to people who would reject them on account of ageing. The image of the traditional 'old' seems to promise a return to a comforting, stable and idyllic past; he/she is seen as the repository of old values and ways of life and is linked to a more "genuine" cultural identity. Some societies venerate age, equating it with wisdom. In spite of the various cultural revolutions in China, a positive value is still placed upon old age. The traditional Chinese culture looks upon the aged as being one step from the gods, as being a repository of wisdom and knowledge, and as meriting an attitude of reverence (Linton, 1942).

However, a study of villages in India indicates that although respect for old age is still espoused as an ideal, the reality in everyday life may be very different (Harlan, 1968).

Old age is often portrayed as the drab and dismal terminal period of human existence. We should remember two characteristics of human development in assessing ageing. First, the aged person will be more or less the same as he was when a younger adult¾personality usually does not change drastically. Thus, adjustment to old age can usually be predicted from previous functioning. Second, certain conditions promote successful ageing¾especially physical health and an income adequate to maintain a way of life resembling that of the earlier adult years. Other important factors are a range of skills and interests so that life is considered rewarding, an intact and generally happy marriage, and satisfying ties to children and other relatives. Many older people can fulfil these conditions. As a result they can add life to the years and find ageing a time of great satisfaction (Brieland et al., 1975).

The elderly in pre-industrial societies were not systematically assigned a prestigious status, nor was value always attached to their wisdom and experience. Although industrialization tended to reduce old people's social status, this does not hold equally true for all social classes.

On the other hand, for many, old age is synonymous with disability. This disability could be any one or a combination of these¾physical, social, cognitive, instrumental or even perceived—and very often inhibits an individual in performing his daily activities.

Old conjures many negative images. Old age is also depicted negatively in terms of decline in physical attractiveness, vigour, health conditions, sexual prowess. and perhaps some mental abilities, and decrepitude. Elderly people are perceived as persons on the decline, seemingly incapable of renewal and growth. They are characterized or stereotyped as ill, tired, mentally slow, self-pitying, not sexually interested, unhappy and unproductive. They are often depressed by feelings of loneliness and alienation. An individual who withdraws from social contacts, for whatever reasons, will find himself increasingly isolated and unfulfilled. The probability that he will spend his remaining years in loneliness and sadness increases. Some scholars point out that negative images of ageing as a psychological process of decline are socially constructed. The negative content of the condition of old age derives from the relationship of individuals and society; the absence of a role, the isolation from significant social life, the marginality in family relationships, and the lack of commitment, partly induced, partly forced on old people. With increasing age, the anticipated life span fore-shortened, requiring constant readjustment in the allocation of time, effort and other resources. Second, older persons tend to be perceived—and often perceive themselves—as not having sufficient futurity to deserve a major investment of the resources of others, such as the state, the family, the community, the work organization and so forth. Decreasing mobility, detachment and dislocation from community institutions and break up of the family represents old age.

Strategy

In formulating any approach for the care of the elderly, it is important to bear in mind that they are not a homogeneous group. Their problems and needs vary and can be considered under three headings - financial, health and socio-psychological. These problems are interdependent. For instance, if an elderly person is poor, his health may be affected because of his inability to purchase medicines or to have a nutritious diet.

Financial problems: In a country like India, where two-fifths of the population is below the poverty line, a large number of persons in old age are left with very inadequate incomes. There are a number of women, who have only been housewives and have never been workers, whether in wage employment or in self-employment. There are men, who have been agricultural workers or employed in lowly paid jobs, or been self-employed, all providing meager earnings. And there may be persons who have been working in the organized sector but are now retired and have to live on reduced incomes. Some studies have indicated that within about five years after retirement, a large number among them exhaust their savings and become dependent on their children or relatives. Pensioners are another vulnerable group whose earnings are affected by inflation. An organized group of pensioners can bring pressure on the government for fully neutralizing the increase in the cost of living. Another problem group is that of the destitute elderly. Although State governments have evolved schemes for the destitute elderly, their implementation is far from satisfactory. The bureaucratic hurdles are enormous and many eligible persons are not registered under the scheme. There is need to carry out surveys and gather factual information about the magnitude of the problem.

Health problems: It is a biological fact that when one becomes old, health and vigour decline. There are, however, individual differences here. Some individuals continue to enjoy good health even in old age whereas others have poor health even in their forties and fifties. Studies have shown that there are some ailments which are more common among elderly people (asthma, rheumatism, etc.). In very old age, difficulties are experienced in carrying out day-to-day activities. Therefore, the very old have to lead restricted lives. Some suggestions are made here to minimize the sufferings of the elderly in availing medical facilities. Hospitals and public dispensaries are usually over-crowded and persons have to wait in queues for a long time. Separate queues for the elderly will be of great help. The elderly patient is most likely to experience transportation difficulties in going from his residence to hospitals and back. One can think of organizing such a facility. The elderly may require some aids to lead a normal life such as spectacles, hearing aids and crutches. One can even think in terms of a health visitor or a nurse who can make home visits and help the elderly in coping with health problems. Old persons also require medicines, vitamins and tonics at subsidized cost to maintain their health. Many elderly persons need advice on how to maintain their health.

Socio-psychological problems: In the past the elderly were respected for their capacity and wisdom. Now the situation has changed in many ways, and the elderly do not get the respect they deserve. In a large number of cases their presence is tolerated; they are often not treated well. Those, who can afford, do not, therefore, want to stay with their children or relatives. This is also reciprocated by the young who want to establish their own households and leave the old people to fend for themselves. This unfortunate situation can be mitigated by the elderly themselves to some extent. As a group they can think of some socially useful activities and implement them. Individually, they can be useful to their family members. With more women seeking and securing employment, the help of the elderly is needed in a home where both husband and wife are working. Grandparents can look after the children, help them with their school lessons and assist in shopping and in light domestic work. Retired people can also take up some problems faced by the community which need to be sorted out at the level of the Government or the local authorities.

The psychological problems faced by the elderly can be a matter of great concern. Failing health, continuing ailments, poor financial situation and humiliation in the family can all add up to feelings of helplessness, hopelessness, depression and anxiety. Such persons need assistance. It is here that groups of the elderly can provide company, solace and help. In every community the elderly should be encouraged to form associations which can plan activities which are useful to the community and demonstrate to others that they are still useful citizens. A day for the elderly can be observed in the same manner as children's day or teacher's day to focus the attention of society on the needs of the elderly.

Successful Ageing

Marjatta in her paper "Successful Ageing Dependent on Cultural Social Capital?" (2001) opines that the increase of elderly population has aroused discussions and debates on several age-generation-related issues, such as political, social, cultural and medical. The idea behind this is to tackle with changing position of elderly people in society, especially concerning their power and autonomy. It also deals with the cultural and social resources the elderly people have in the modern society. The viewpoint arises from Pierre Bowrdieu's theories, which deal with different kinds of resources (capital) that influence people's position in power structures and social life. Three different kinds of capital are important when dealing with successful ageing and well being: Cultural, Social and Symbolical. Though economic capital plays an important part in this respect it is seen more dependent on the other three than as an independent resource. The social capital comprises, for instance, social networks, organizations, family etc. and the norms, rights and obligations arising from them. Social capital is also the source of symbolic capital. The capital is needed in legitimizing the value and importance and social meaning of other forms of capital. These values are the targets of negotiations and fights that take place in social interaction. The cultural capital, the easier it is for him/her to own symbolic power in social interaction.

Successful ageing can be taken from the viewpoint of society and individual. It is born and created in the interaction between these two in a certain cultural setting. Thus successful ageing cannot be totally individual or social and its features are dependent on both levels, what is successful from society's point of view, may not be successful to individuals, what is successful in certain culture, may not be successful in another, and what is successful for one person may not be successful to another. It should also be noted that, as a concept, successful ageing contains more than mere healthy ageing.

Notwithstanding, the modern society denies the value of the cultural capital of elderly people. By this devaluation, the symbolic power of the elderly people as a group diminishes. The present mechanisms of symbolic capital tend to legitimize mainly the work-related, active mid life position and activities. They also seem to emphasise the value of social capital leaning only on these qualities. Thus, they operate as lessening the social capital of the elderly. Their own social activities and networks are losing their symbolic value. Through these processes the elderly population are divided by gender, the activities and networks typical to women's life course are undermined, and a retirement may become too big a change to men.

Successful Ageing

Marjatta in her paper "Successful Ageing Dependent on Cultural Social Capital?" (2001) opines that the increase of elderly population has aroused discussions and debates on several age-generation-related issues, such as political, social, cultural and medical. The idea behind this is to tackle with changing position of elderly people in society, especially concerning their power and autonomy. It also deals with the cultural and social resources the elderly people have in the modern society. The viewpoint arises from Pierre Bowrdieu's theories, which deal with different kinds of resources (capital) that influence people's position in power structures and social life. Three different kinds of capital are important when dealing with successful ageing and well being: Cultural, Social and Symbolical. Though economic capital plays an important part in this respect it is seen more dependent on the other three than as an independent resource. The social capital comprises, for instance, social net works, organizations, family etc and the norms, rights and obligations arising from them. Social capital is also the source of symbolic capital. The capital is needed in legitimizing the value and importance and social meaning of other forms of capital. These values are the targets of negotiations and fights that take place in social interaction. The cultural capital, the easier it is for him/her to own symbolic power in social interaction.

Successful ageing can be taken from the view point of society and individual. It is born and created in the interaction between these two in a certain cultural setting. Thus successful ageing cannot be totally individual or social and its features are dependent on both levels, what is successful from society's point of view, may not be successful to individuals, what is successful in certain culture, may not be successful in another, and what is successful for one person may not be successful to another. It should also be noted that, as a concept, successful ageing contains more than mere healthy ageing.

Notwithstanding, the modern society denies the value of the cultural capital of elderly people. By this devaluation, the symbolic power of the elderly people as a group diminishes. The present mechanisms of symbolic capital tend to legitimize mainly the work-related, active mid life position and activities. They also seem to emphasise the value of social capital leaning only on these qualities. Thus, they operate as lessening the social capital of the elderly. Their own social activities and networks are losing their symbolic value. Through these processes the elderly population are divided by gender, the activities and networks typical to women's life course are undermined, and a retirement may become too big a change to men.

5

Senior Citizens

The advent of new technology, life-saving drugs, better knowledge of health and nutrition, and effective treatment of diseases have increased life expectancy, delayed the onset of old age and its attendant health problems and mitigated suffering. This inevitably has resulted in an increase in the number of senior citizens and, in its trail, several problems have emerged imposing a great strain on their families as well as society, not excluding the State, particularly in the opulent West. The developing countries including India give little attention to the problems of the aged though they display a profusion of sympathy for them.

Barely two decades ago centenarians were few in number. Now their number is increasing at a fast pace in the developed countries. Even in developing countries like India the problem has begun to be felt and one should not be surprised if shortly one in every five families has a third and fourth generation, which phenomenon, though impressive is likely to impose great strain on families. The grandfathers and great grandfathers may witness this with mixed feelings of pleasure and pain—pleasure because of the happy new arrival and pain because the elder cannot yield place to the youngest. This causes tension because of limited housing, restricted resources and mounting expenses.

In developed countries the family, society and the government realized the need for caring for the aged long ago. In America, Senior Citizens Centres have come up al over the country, providing a variety of services. Voluntary organizations and government agencies work hand in hand to organize and support programmes for the care of the aged.

In India it is necessary to draw up a plan of action and implement it. This would be a better way of helping senior citizens than gratuitous advice and lip sympathy, or the offer of dole whi9ch they may detest, because not so long before they were able-bodied, respectable citizens winning bread for their families and looking after themselves with respect and dignity. Hence the task of helping the aging is delicate because the recipients of help are very sensitive. The programme to assist the aging can be achieved through:

(i) Cooperation from the family with its aging members;
(ii) Counselling from the society with senior citizens centres offering guidance on all matters;
(iii) Help from the government, special amenities and concessions; and
(iv) The aging helping themselves.

Role of Family

It behaves every family to look after its aging members and make them feel that they are not unwanted but are an integral part of the family. The elderly members, if convinced of this intention and attitude on the part of the younger members of the family, would really feel relieved and consoled. On their part, they should overlook minor shortcomings and domestic irritants and assist in the smooth running of the family, in however small a measure. An elderly person can do a variety of things at home such as maintaining cleanliness, attending to the garden, doing shopping, entertaining children, taking them round for strolls, guiding them in their growth and helping them at homework.

Neighbourhood and Society

The neighbourhood in particular, and society in general, can play an important role in the life of the senior citizen and make it worth living. Likeminded elderly persons can form groups and develop common hobbies and play games of common interest. Their services can be utilized by schools and colleges, and social and commercial institutions. There are innumerable activities like guiding the unemployed, helping the disabled, tree-planting activity, tuitions to poor students, and adult literacy programmes which may even bring monetary returns besides the pleasure of helping the needy which can be very rewarding.

Government's Duty Towards Senior Citizens

The Government can take a number of steps to ameliorate the conditions of the aging who are the senior citizens. Persons taking care of aged relations should be entitled to rebates in income tax. Free insurance cover should be provided to senior citizens against accidents and for health care. It is regrettable that very little has been done for senior citizens by the Government, the plea usually advanced being paucity of funds. Senior citizens can ill afford to agitate; therefore, they have to resort to fact the persuasion, to influence policy-makers to give a higher priority to the care of the aged than in the past. The Government should allot suitable plots of land free of cost where geriatric services can be provided. Gerontologists and geriatric experts from abroad can, in the initial stages, provide guidance in the organization of services in the senior citizens centres as some countries have a much wider experience in this regard; however, local needs and the socio-cultural frame-work have to be kept in view. Senior officers in Government or those who have retired from high positions can be very effective in influencing Government decision-making, which will be of advantage to the aged; they can also be helpful in securing grants-in-aid.

Senior Citizens Helping Themselves

Having religious moorings and a philosophical outlook, Indians generally believe in the theory of Karma. The aged have all along been accepting the ups and downs of life with a shrug of their shoulders and meekly tolerating the ravages of old age without doing anything to avoid them. This is more so in backward areas. Enlightened people have realized, however, that they can live the rest of their lives in a purposeful and peaceful manner. The aging should, in the first instance, convince themselves that they should be fully concerned about their health, take pre ventive care and adapt their life-style to their health status. They should not believe in the statement that old age is synonymous with dependency and ill-health, or that age deprives the person of much of his mental capacity and productive abilities. There are innumerable examples from all over the world of great things being achieved after the age of 60. John Milton wrote his paradise regained when he was blind and old. Churchill directed the forces of the Allies and won historic victories over the Nazis at an age when most people retire and relax. Evan his memoirs of the war, written later, made literary history. So also, the contributions of George Bernard Shaw, Ernest Hemingway, Benjamin Franklin, Rabindranath Tagore and C.V. Raman have been monumental.

Senior Citizens

The term 'Senior Citizens' is many times used loosely. Since it is necessary that it convey the same meaning to all, it is proposed to define it. Commensurate with our scriptures and traditions the elderly persons are expected to playa role in the society. It is reasonable to assume that this role be played for at least last 5 years if not 10 years of ones life. Considering the vast population of India, and the longevity of an average man was 60 years in the year 2000, it may be prudent to consider every individual of 55 years age and above should be considered as a "Senior Citizen".

This matter was discussed and agreed upon in the SAARC Nations Consultation on Ageing for all the developing countries. This conference was held in Pune on 17th to 19th August 2001. The matter has also beeen projected to the Chairman National Commission to Review Working of the Constitution for consideration and has been pursued from beginning of the year 2000.

Objectives for Mobilization

Through the "National Policy on the Elderly" as well as the "Five Year Action Plan 2000 to 2005" do not identify the Objectives of the either, one may assume that they desire to ensure "Graceful Ageing" for all the elderly. Taking suitable clues from the scriptures and the fact that the following generations look up to them as "Role Models" the objectives could be identified as under.

Personal Level

- Lead healthy, satisfying and productive retired life
- Be self-sufficient and self-reliant.
- Study, promote and preserve rich Indian culture.

Family Level

- Ensure family harmony and family concept.
- Promote cultural values and norms.
- Act as a valuable resource to family members when the need arises.

Social Level

- Provide support to needy Senior Citizens.
- Help build up a strong social fiber.
- Productive participation in the governance of the country al all levels.

The purpose of mobilizing the Senior Citizens cannot be different!

Assessment of Resources

Assessment of resources is essential to determine the dimensions of the extra effort required as against the capacities and limitations of the NGO bodies considered for mobilization.

Man Power

The most Abundant, Knowledgeable, Experienced and Mature Human resource, in terms of Senior Citizens (Sr. Cits.), is available but is hardly utilized. Harnessing this resource may appear to be a most challenging job, but for a developing country like India, with its high moral and cultural traditions, it cannot be an impossible job. It may have to be a major revolution on the social front but with the financial crunch it may well be unavoidable. Experience has shown that the basic fact the 'Man is a social animal' can be a very useful tool. The available human resource is probably of little use as individuals. When this resource is available in a united form or in an organized fashion it can be a major self-sufficient tool which can be used to a great advantage. Pune situation provides a model for this purpose. It is natural for the senior citizens to get together and once in a group, it is natural for them to get in an activity mode. This natural phenomenon can be used to get in an activity mode. This natural phenomenon can be used to a great advantage. A revolution of sorts is already taking place in the metropolis of Mumbai and Pune, which are also acting, like laboratories for experimenting "Practical Gerontology". These Sr. Cits. Orgs.

Must maintain a character tree from political bias. In practice it has been found that Sr. Cits'. Orgs. Are uniquely Mutually Self Supporting in character who can raise resources on their own. It may take a revolution to set this trend but for India it is vita.

Finance

The most vital but most scarce resource is finance. For a developing country like India, it can pose a problem if the meager funds available are not judiciously utilized. The finances should be mainly used to create infrastructures to bring medical care with in affordable reach to the elderly in all strata of the society. Funds may also be needed for providing accommodation for Day-Care-Centers, offices of the apex bodies of Senior Citizens Organizations, Gerontology and Geriatric Research Establishments, Data Collection Centers etc. Following sources of funds can be tapped for the purpose:

- Percentages of budget allotments of various concerned ministries
- Corporate sector including financial institutions may be encouraged to provide for setting up some support facilities.
- Contributions and donations from individuals, foundations, trusts etc.,
- Enterprises run by the Sr. Cits. Orgs, preferably on co-operative basis, can generate funds and also provide second careers for the needy.
- Funds from socially oriented organizations like helpmate, Rotary Clubs, Lions Clubs and others.

Government Initiatives

The Government at the center has the prime responsibility to lay down definitions, general strategies and policy guidelines. In addition identifying long-term and short term measures, ensuring awareness, laying down time bound objectives apart from budget allocations are resource by themselves.

The State Government initiatives can also act as a rich resource. Finalizing suitable state policies, making suitable legislations, amending various byelaws, award of concessions for projects for the cause of the Sr.Cits. etc. can lead to promotion and generation of suitable facilities and infrastructures with the use of local resources.

Other Agencies

Corporate sector, Public trusts and foundations, Financial institutions, NGOs are all important resource who can undertake socially oriented programmes for the cause of the Senior Citizens.

Utiliazation of Resources

Identifying resources alone is not sufficient. Judicious utilization is also equally responsible for implementing the measures planned. Health aspects being given the priority, it shall be prudent to allocate maximum funds to create country wide infrastructures in a phased manner. Since these infrastructures will be equally useful to the entire population, Planning Commission should undertake these issues if they are not already doing it. Public audit of such planned efforts can help to build general confidence. The Government must decide to concentrate on health issue by earmarking maximum efforts for it. Other aspects like housing, old age pensions, etc., cannot be ensured for al the deserving casers and at present are being made available only at selected places. This withers our funds and nothing substantial is achieved.

Mechanics of Mobilization

In the present day circumstances general tendency amongst elders from all strata of the society is to avoid volunteering for almost any cause. This is particularly so when there is no monetary incentive. This makes the task of motivation that much difficult. However experience shows it is not impossible. Indirect awareness campaigns, personal contacts,. Media publicity, etc are some of the methods, which may be slow in the beginning but they catch-up in due course of time. The character of "Senior Citizens Movement" is that of a "Social Revolution". Unless carefully cultivated it may not result in the desired NGO infrastructure. This calls for laying down some parameters or Terms of Reference as a guide.

Terms of Reference

- "Senior Citizen": Every individual of 55 years of age or more is considered as a "Senior Citizen" and is expected to playa positive role in the society. This status is independent of caste, creed, religion, financial status, educational status, and political bias.
- For viable results working of senior citizens in groups or as an organization is essential.
- The character of such groups or organizations shall be tree from any political bias
- These organizations should chase social goals in particular for the cause of the elderly.

Motivation

The first step is to get individuals with initiative, attracted and exposed to the need for a Senior Citizens' Movement. This may be possible by employing one or more or similar other measures suggested as under.

- Write articles in the local news papers and magazines giving contact addresses and phone numbers.
- Use radio9 and TV media to publicize the cause of the elderly and the best way to achieve it.

- Participate in local "Public Lecture Series" organized by various NGOs or educational institutes.
- Get the local government involved in the process as a social venture.
- Organize competitions for posters, essays, etc to get the local senior citizens involvement. Local government, corporate sector or even individual philanthropists may sponsor this.

The Aged and Society

One of the major responsibilities of civilized societies is to take care of their vulnerable groups. The aged are one such group. As the individual grows older (specially beyond 65 years) his health begins to decline. At an advanced age, an individual may not be able to take care of himself in day-to-day life. He may also become financially dependent because he may not be able to earn his livelihood; and large numbers from the disadvantaged sections of society do not have savings to fall back upon. An old person may become socially vulnerable because he may find that his status in society has declined, and in his own family he may not receive the same importance. He may become psychologically vulnerable and experience loneliness, and may even become senile at a later age. He may be subject to the stress of anxiety over his future—failing health, declining mental abilities, depleted financial resources and the care and attention he will have at the time of his death.

It is not suggested that all the aged become vulnerable and, therefore, are in need of help. Some of the aged may continue to be healthy and self-reliant. Some of them may retain their financial independence, their social status and their psychological abilities. But many may not be so fortunate and would require assistance in a variety of ways. It is necessary to identify the aged who are in need of help and then make arrangements to extend services to them.

The matters which exercise our policy-makers and receive priority are agriculture, industry and power. There are other priorities too, such, as children who constitute about 40 per cent of the population; and the vast numbers of unemployed and under-employed youth. The situation of the elderly in the developed countries has been somewhat different as policy-makers are to some extent attuned to their problems.

The proportion of the elderly in developed countries being much higher, they are politically important as a group and are able to exert pressure on the State to allocate more resources for their care. The elderly in developing countries are proportionally less in number, and are not organized and therefore, politically ineffective as a pressure group. Their problems are likely to be accorded a low priority by the government. Therefore, an important role will have to be played by voluntary organizations to fill the big gap in services. One of the first requirements is to organize the elderly across the country into associations. This is a Herculean task but beginnings have to be made. In Maharashtra there is already a federation of organizations of the elderly spread all over the

Table: Percentage Column-wise Distribution of the Elderly by Marital Status

Marital Status	*Male*	*Female*	*Total*
Never married	3.3(5)	1.3(2)	2.3(7)
Currently married	60.0(90)	30.0(45)	45.0(135)
Widowed	36.7(55)	67.4(101)	52.0(156)
Divorced/ Separated	-	1.3(2)	0.7(2)
Total	100.0(150)	100.0(150)	100.0(300)

state. One can think of such State federations elsewhere too and then form a national confederation of the elderly.

The associations of the elderly should organize various activities which would be useful and sustain the interests of the members; they should centre round identified problems and needs. There should be adequate information about the problems of the aged; voluntary organizations can select some of these and organize services.

The predominant proportion of widows (67.4%) indicates greater mortality among male elderly which is quite natural being much older than their wives because of the Indian tradition of marrying a bride who is several years younger to the bridegroom.

In general, the old age is accompanied by a decline in economic status. However, neither all the aged people are living in the same economic condition, nor are they adversely affected in the same way or to the same extent always. The variations in economic conditions mainly depend upon marital status of the person (Vijaya Kumar 1991, p-77). In old age, the marital statuses such as Never-Married, Currently married, Widowed

Table Working and Non-working Elderly by marital Status

Marital Status	*Working*	*Not working*	*Total*
Never married	42.9(3)	57.1(4)	2.3(7)
Currently married	32.6(44)	67.4(91)	45.0(135)
Widowed	21.2(33)	78.8(123)	52.0(156)
Divorced/ Separated	-	100.0(2)	0.7(2)
Total	26.7(80)	73.3(220)	100.0(300)

$X^2 = 6.5141$; dt = 3, p. = 0.0891 (Percentages are row-wise)

and Divorced/Separated place elderly in general and women in particular in a more disadvantaged position in the society and they live as dependents for a long time.

A large majority of the widowed elderly (78.8%) and divorced/separated (100.0%) were not economically active which means widowed and divorced/separated withdraw themselves from active labour force compared to the never married and currently married and in this process their physical and mental strength gradually decreases. Consequently, they may not be able to perform certain roles and works which they were previously performing. Such inability decreases their earning capacity and eventually they are forced to depend upon the other members of the family and lose their economic independence. The chi-square test result does not show significant association between marital status and working and non-working status.

In general, aged people tend to have low income and little accumulated wealth, and as a result, many of them are in a poor position to maintain even the optimum standards of food, clothing, housing and other social amenities.

Table Percentage (Row-wise) Distribution of Elderly by Own House

Marital Status	*Having own house*	*Having own house*	*Total*
Never married	85.7(6)	14.3(1)	100.0(7)
Currently married	88.1(119)	11.9(16)	100.00(135)
Widowed	57.1(89)	42.9(67)	100.0(156)
Divorced/ Separated	50.0(1)	50.0(1)	100.00(2)
Total	71.7(215)	28.3(85)	100.00(300)

$X^2 = 35.61321$; df = 3; p = 0.000

A majority of the widowed (42.9) and divorced/separated were found to be not having own house as compared to never married (14.3) and currently married (11.9). Chi-square test result shows a highly significant association between marital status and owning a house.

6

Collective Approach of Senior Citizens

1. Comprehensive Approach

The obvious needs of elderly persons are related to income, housing, access to service and medical aid. Other needs which characterize the elderly are social protection, prevention of diseases and psycho-social support. They also have higher order needs like self-esteem. A sense of identity. Recognition and respect from the young ones. Complete health of an elder, therefore, includes physical, social and mental well-being. This is strongly influenced by nutrition, psychological make up of the aged, particularly his attitudes, desire to seek information and share experiences. These contribute to his adjustment. Isolation and loneliness add to his mental and physical decline. Social contact and stimulation including the ability to return favours, to serve society even in small ways help maintain self-esteem. With advancing age. Many dysfunctions become increasingly noticeable. At the same time motives like self-actualisation and acceptance become urgent . Single source of support is inadequate. There is a need to integrate various services available for elderly people to ensure that the components function as a true system rather than as a series of compartments operating in a manner that may not fit well with those of others. Achieving and maintaining high standards of care depend on continuing comprehensive efforts by the concerned parties – the family, the community and the state. Community and government support cannot be effective without the informal care provided by family, neighbours and friends. This informal care needs to be coordinated with community services, volunteers play a vital role in supplementing such services. Senior citizens' associations can help organize formal, informal and voluntary services at the local level. When seniors themselves act as volunteers, service can be quick and effective.

Demographic changes in the family structure due to urbanization, industrialization, and economic recession have resulted in changes in value systems, sentiments, behaviour patterns and lifestyles. Younger members of a family find it difficult to meet their obligations to the aged. Still family is the main emotional as well as social support. In their study Jamuna and Ramamurti, found most children of aging parents viewing care of the elderly as their duty and obligation because parents reared them, educated them and it is customary to do so. Most of the elders also felt so and they often expected children to take care of them in their old age. However, all the problems and issues of caring were not viewed similarly by the elderly and their care-giving youngsters. There was some disparity between the expectations of the elderly and their perception of performance by their children. More women than men expressed greater affection for their parents. Similarly many elderly felt more comfortable with their daughters than with their married sons.

Unfortunately, in our culture the daughter-in-law and mother-in-law look at each other with the traditional stigma and prejudice, the caring of the elderly mother-in-law to a greater extent, and the elderly father-in-law to a greater extent, and the elderly father-in-law to a lesser extent, is tinged with strain and dislike. As a result, the caring functions suffer in many cases quality wise. The situation was even worse where the mother-in-law was widowed and if she had behaved authoritatively and vin-dictively towards the daughter-in-law in the past. If the elderly were staying with the married daughter, and where the son-in-law's parents were not interfering with the arrangements and creating open conflicts, the elderly lead a comfortable living. Thus, in-law equations become very significant factors in the caring of the elderly in India (Jamuna, 1990; Ramamurti, et al, 1991). In the light of the in-law problems, plenty of intervention programmes are needed to educate through family counselling and use of the powerful visual media to project non stereotype to typical relationship between them and promote better interrelationships between daughter-in-law and mother-in-law. An understanding mother-in-law and a co-operative daughter-in-law can make care of the aged at home a very effective and pleasant interaction. Accommodation, expressive concern and mutual help go a long way in promoting good interpersonal relationships.

India should learn much from the experience of developed countries in the field of social assistance and social security programmes, the special schemes for the aged with regard to housing, health, education and recreation, the institutional arrangements for the aged, the automatic procedures for safeguarding the real income of the pensioners against the onslaught of inflation and a host of related issues. It has to fight for the emancipation of women who remain at a disadvantage, right from birth to death. The plight of widows is particularly deplorable. It is not enough to give pension to the organized sector of the labour force and leave out much larger agricultural sector from social protection through state assistance. The landless workers in agriculture and the urban workers in the unorganized sector constitute the bulk of the poor in India. They need to be provided with social assistance and social security on priority basis.

India cannot afford to opt for a system of expensive total institutional care for the aged as is commonly found in the west. The country has to develop an integrated system of supporting the elderly which combines the features of both developed and developing countries. The following are some of the useful ideas, which need further scrutiny. The concept of care should include the whole family – parents, children, adolescent with provision for ailing elders within a home and familial setting. Although ailing elders have the same care needs as the rest of the population, their ailment is likely to be chronic, multiple and prolonged. Therefore in addition to normal care, treatment of the aged should be aimed at prevention and atleast postponement of disability. In addition to medicines, they need social and psychological support. To retain and reinforce the family ties, the community organizations have to counsel the aged. Government can help the families with elderly by sanctioning reasonable amount of money by way of old age benefits. The institutional care should be used only when it is inevitable.

Need for Data on the Elderly

Very scanty information is available on the situation of the elderly in different strata of society. Very few studies have been done on the needs and problems of the elderly in rural areas and urban slums and of elderly widows and widowers even from the relatively better off sections of society. The National Sample Survey Organisation conducted a national survey in 1986-87 but it has to be followed up by more detailed empirical studies. The information thus made available will not only enable a proper diagnosis of the situation to be met but also help in formulating policies and programmes which are based on services they really need. There are, for instance cases where old age homes have been constructed at places where there is little need for them. Such situations could have been avoided if a survey was done beforehand to find out if such a home was needed.

Globalisation and the Aged

The concept of globalization is one that has become widely used in debates, in politics, business and media over the past few years. A decade ago, the term 'globalization' was relatively unknown. Today it seems to be on the top of everyone's tongue. Globalization refers to the fact that we are all increasingly living in 'one world', so that individuals, groups and nations become more interdependent.

Sociologists use the term globalization to refer to those processes, which are intensifying worldwide social relations and interdependence. It is a social phenomenon with vast implications, it should not be thought of simply as the development of worldwide networks—social and economic systems that are remote from out individual concerns. It is a local phenomena too, one that affects all of us in our daily lives. It is changing the way the world looks, and the way we look at the world. By adopting a global outlook, we become more aware of out connections to people in other societies. We also become more conscious of the many problems the world faces at the start of the twenty first century. The global perspective opens our eyes to the fact that our increasing ties with the rest of the world means that our actions have consequences for others and that the world's problems have consequences for us.

Globalisation – its Meaning

Anthony Giddens, in a book on the Edge: Living with Global Capitalism identifies many meanings of globalization; firstly as:

(i) The world wide communication revolution

(ii) Secondly, he refers to what he terms the 'weightless economy'; by this he means the new 'knowledge economy' , with financial markets at its leading edge.

(iii) Thirdly, it refers to a post – 1988 world, that is world after the fall of communism and

(iv) Fourthly, it refers to transformations happening on the level of everyday life.

Globalization – Its Impact on Aged

A general concern about the worldwide phenomena of increase in the aged population has existed for many years now. On the global level the phenomena of population ageing was first highlighted in 1982 when the United Nations organized the first world conference on ageing in Vienna. In the present times the proportion of people who are sixty-five or over is steadily increasing. At the same time, the issue of the social importance of ageing is one that ranges much more broadly. For what old age actually in – the opportunities it offers and the burdens it carries – is changing dramatically. Gerontology, the study of ageing and the elderly, concerns itself not only with the physical process of growing old, but also with social and cultural factors concerned to ageing.

Two rather contradictory processes are involved here. On the one hand, older people in modern societies tend to have lower status and less power than they used to have in pre-modern culture. In these cultures, as in non-western societies today, old age was believed to bring wisdom, and the older people in any given community were commonly its main decision-makers. Today, increasingly age normally brings with it something of its reverse. In a society undergoing constant change, as ours is, the accumulated knowledge of older people often seems to the young no l0onger valuable store of wisdom, but simply behind the times.

On the other hand, however older people today are much less prone to accept ageing as inevitable process of the decay of the body. Here once more we can trace the impact of the nature of socialization. The ageing process was once generally accepted as an inevitable manifestation of the ravages of time. But increasingly, ageing is not something taken for granted as natural. Advances in medicines and nutrition have shown that much that was once regarded as inevitable about ageing can either be countered or slowed down. On average, people live to much older ages than was true over a century ago, as a result of improvements in nutrition hygiene and health care.

Globalization is a complex process, which has diverse meanings and facts. These meanings are important. Challenges of globalization are (a) economic and (b) social, leading to marginalization of the aged. Retrenchment of personnel and its implications for the aged and in terms of certain kind of positive and negative freedom, new opportunities in terms of the potential for self fulfillment.

Development of the Aged People - Strategies and Approaches

In the light of the findings of the study it is understood that the problems of the aged get accentuated by poverty and also by the extent and nature of changes in family relationships. The old age in India may correspond with the processes of isolation, disengogement, lack of social activity, and role flexibility. Among the aged population the widowed, divorced/ separated, non-working, and dependent elderly are the worst sufferers. The social security measures for the rural aged particularly for the deprived of the deprived aged are either meager or completely lacking. There is a felt need for social work intervention with the rural aged particularly with their families facing problems of poverty, low income, indebtedness and unemployment. The elderly in the advanced years of the age are not able to work and earn an income, and hence, they have to depend on the earning members of their families. In certain instances the poor and low income families are not able to support their elderly members. The conditions of widows, divorced/separated and the non-working elderly members are deplorable. Empowerment of the deprived elderly may be undertaken by professional Social Workers and N.G.Os by starting production centers, agricultural co-operatives, self-help, thrift and saving groups. Their expertise and rich experience may be utilized by promiting their participation in the socio-economic development of the nation. The professional social workers play an important role for strengthening the families by motivating people to fulfill their responsibilities to the elderly. Counseling services for the families and the elderly people may be rendered for dealing with the psycho-social problems of the aged persons. It is quite appropriate for the social work profession to devote its time and attention for overall social development and social rights issues concerning the elderly population who are deprived of familial care and community attention in both the developing and under developed countries as well.

Employment Opportunities for Senior Citizens Pose Problems on Following Accounts

- The retiring population may not be physically in a position to undertake a fulltime job nor may be able to commute over long distances for the same.
- The new procedures and modern techniques may have made their skills outdated.
- The corporate sector managerial cadres are scheduled to retire at an earlier age as compared to the retiring age as laid down by the Government. This is likely to reduce the chances for the elderly to seek second careers. The voluntary retirement schemes in Government and semi

Government establishments have further added to the numbers seeking second careers.

- Status mania amongst the middle classes has been found to promote lifestyles beyond the actual financial status during service. This leads even to avoiding low paid jobs and endure financial crunch.
- Amongst those who have managed to find a job or to continue in their old professions, many do not know when to retire. Only medical problems make them stop. These cases find it very difficult to adjust with the home environments.
- In the rural areas again there are no such opportunities for second career nor can they till the lands on their own or work as laborers on account of declining physical standards.

7

Eneravated Approach of Senior Citizens

The Economic Myth

It is widely believed that majority of older persons are poor and economically dependent. "Not having enough honey to live on" was considered a problem for older persons by 62 percent of the public, but only 15 percent of seniors thought is a problem (Harris, 1976). This myth has divesting consequences for any person approaching retirement and may lead to negative attitude on the part of their children. The myth results in a distorted picture of our older population, gives them a poor public image, and makes adaptation difficult for the aged. The myth that most older persons are unable to work because of weakness, physical problems, mental illness, senility and so forth is often cited to justify mandatory retirement at sixty years in India and sixty five in developed countries. The economic myth says that older persons are poor because they deserve to be poor. But on the contrary great majority of old persons, males and females could contribute to the economic progress of the country. The following table depict the work status among the various groups of aged in this study.

Table : Working Status of the Aged

Marital Status	*Working*	*Not working*	*Total*
Never married	42.9(3)	57.1(4)	2.3(7)
Currently married	32.6(44)	67.4(91)	45.0(135)
Widowed	21.2(33)	78.8(123)	52.0(156)
Divorced/ Separated	-	100.0(2)	0.7(2)
Total	26.7(80)	73.3(220)	100.0(300)

$X^2 = 6.51421$; df = 3; p = 0.0891 (Percentages among categories are row-wise and among totals are table-wise)

It is clear from the above table that a substantial percentage (73.3%) of the aged persons were found to be non working while only 26.7% percent of the aged were working. Among the non-working aged, divorced/separated (100%) occupied first place followed by widowed (78.8%), currently married (67.4%) and never married (57.1%). Among working aged, 42.9 percent were never married and none from the divorced or separated category was found working. However, Chi-square test value does not show a significant association between marital status and working status. In total, most of the aged (7.3%) were found to be non working while more than a quarter of them could work. The reason could be that despite their interest and ability of doing certain works, most of the aged were being rejected and isolated from works. The disengagement theory supports this view and it explains that society tends unilaterally to isolate or reject the old, that individuals in the later years themselves begin to limit their activities and that they literally begin to disengage themselves from the mainstream of life in preparation for the end and in response to a lower level of energy (Cumming and Henry, 1961).

The Health Myth

The myth about health adds anxiety to the way older persons view themselves and the years they have left. Every society usually takes it for granted that the aged persons suffer from some illness or the other and that there is nothing unusual about it. It is surprising that society considers old age as synonymous with sickness. (Shanas, 1968)

Table - Perception of Own Health

Marital Status	*On the whole good*	*Have minor Illness*	*Have serious Illness*	*Total*
Never married	14.3(1)	57.1(4)	28.6(2)	2.3(7)
Currently married	20.0(27)	35.6(48)	44.4(60)	45.0(135)
Widowed	12.8(20)	25.0(39)	62.2(97)	52.0(156)
Divorced/ Separated		50.0(1)	50.0(1)	0.7(2)
Total	16.0(48)	30.7(92)	53.3(160)	100.0(300)

$X^2 = 12.29587$; df = 6; p = 0.0557 (Percentages among categories are row-wise and among totals are table-wise)

The preceding table reveals that majority of the aged (53.3%) were suffering from serious illness, while 30.7 percent were suffering from minor illness. Only 16 percent of the aged perceived that their health on the whole was good. The Chi-square test also shows a marginal association (though not significant) between marital status and perception of own heath. The reason for the illness prevalence among most of the aged could be that whole society is of the view that old age brings with it multiple problems related to health. But this may not necessarily affect functionality in all realms of life. Labeling Theory propounded by Bengston (1973) explains that labels can have a tremendous impact on the way in which we react to others. Once labeled as old, senile, dependent, or sick, the individual will experience a marked reduction in the activities and options of roles. (Bengston, 1973).

The Sexual Myth simply holds that, when men and women reach old age, (the woman after menopause and the man after sixty), nature decrees that sexual drives and responsiveness are gone. This deep-seated myth can destroy that potential and has done so, sad to say, for hundreds of thousands of aging persons (Garden, 1976). Aging virtually is synonymous with physical deterioration, and the effects of prolonged illness leads to intense and unresolved emotional conflicts (Rath, 1989). Sexual myth makes older persons to function below their actual capacity since whole society has false beliefs that old age makes older persons weakened. The theory of Age Stratification model (Riley and Forer, 1972) also explains that age is an important determinant of behaviour for two reasons. First, age may limit the ability of the individual to perform certain roles. Second, society deferentially allocates rights, roles, privileges, and opportunities on the basis of age and individuals' abilities can sometimes modify the impact of age strata.

Mobilizing Senior Citizens for their Own Cause

India is endowed with a very rich cultural heritage. Our scriptures indicate that our forefathers have studied Human Psychology and Ideal Norms to be pursued for leading a Purposeful, Healthy, Comfortale and Happy life in greatest details. These valuable inputs are applicable even in the present day circumstances. The life span catered for in our scriptures appears to be 100 years, The life span is divided in four parts or stages of life. Activities undertaken in these stages in the present day context cou7ld be listed as:

1. **Bramhacarya Ashram:** (Bachelor hood) Period from birth to marriage was considered suitable for acquiring knowledge and is considered as a period of abstinence.
2. **Grihastha Ashram**: (Family Life) Period in one's life from marriage to the time one remains the bread earner and the head of the family.

3. **Vanprastha Ashram**: (Retired Life) Period in life when one has topped or reduced attending to the money earning activities and no more yearns to remain the head of the family. He may continue to stay with the family or stay independently
4. **Sanyasa Ashram**: (Withdrawal from Family) Period in which the individual breaks away from the family and takes refuge in forests or mountains to practice penance.

The latter two stages of life precisely cover the life span from retirement till the end. The scriptures identify how one should lead his life in each of the above four stages of life. The last stage of Sanyassashram is however hardly in practice these days. The scriptures indicate the norms to be followed in terms of following four major parameters:

1. **Aahar :** (Diet) This parameter not only identifies the diet one should follow but also covers the remedies under ayurveda (Herbal medicines) for various ailments.
2. **Vihar :** (Physical Activity) This aspect suggests in what company one may circulate in addition to what activities one should undertake. These also include exercise, yoga, and meditation.
3. **Vichar :** (Line of Thought) Identifying, that the line of thinking plays a major role in the actions (Karma) by every individual, it suggests that Moral and Philosophical reasoning must precede before undertaking any action.
4. **Aachar :** (Conduct) Maximum stress has been given as to how one should conduct oneself in all the phases of one's life.

The above practice can be considered as the fundamental saviour of the Indian culture. Scriptures life "Manusmruti' dwell on these aspects in great detail. It identifies the responsibilities to be fulfilled in the 2nd stage or 'Family Life' and the time one should start migration to the third stage or 'Retirement'.

Indirectly planning for retirement was ensured right from the second stage and chances of 'Graceful Ageing' were almost assured for anyone who cared to follow the norms.

The traditional home caring of the elderly in India worked nicely almost up to seventies. The industrial developments, scientific advances, educational opportunities, better but costly medical facilities etc. all worked towards increasing the cost of living. This prompted younger generations to look for better job opportunities. This resulted in migration of rural youth to towns and cities and also of the urban youth to different parts of the country as well as to the different parts of the world. This affected the traditional norm of the young generation continuing to stay in the parents' house. The change requires the elderly to go and stay with their children. This arrangement is not workable, nor the elderly can move from place to place, thus causing other related problems in maintaining the family harmony. Health status, financial restrictions, changing life styles, values of life, etc., have further added new dimensions to the problems of the older persons. The older persons are no more in a position to offer Knowledge, Experience and Financial backup, as the former two get outdated very fast and the finances are already over stretched. Inadequate living spaces, lack of home care and increasing dependency are reducing the older persons to a nonproductive dependent entity with a great amount of nuisance value.

At the time when the Indian constitution was framed, the elderly population was held in high esteem by one and all. The longevity at birth being very low, the number of the older people was very small and home care by their family members was taken for granted. Perhaps it is for this reason hardly any elaboration appears in the Article 41. Now the time has come to ensure that 'Senior Citizens' and the role they are expected to play are identified in the constitution.

At Pune in Maharashtra, which is considered as a pensioners paradise, considerable activity in terms of the Senior Citizens' Movement has developed over the last 12 years. In the year 1992 there were just 7 Senior Citizens' Organizations functioning in Pune. This number has reached a figure of 78 over the last 10 years and is constantly growing. In the same period the number of Senior Citizens Homes in and around Pune has increased from about 12 to 32. This natural development has lead to considerable interest in these NGOs and their Apex Bodies leading to various studies and surveys to be undertaken. This paper is based on the experiences gained over the last 12 years and brings out how a practical and sound "Social Network" duly supported by Cultural Norms may be developed.

Family System

The "Family system" is a very valued aspect of Indian culture. The old Joint Family system has got modified due to many reasons. Some of the major reasons are as under.

- Family professions not being pursued by the succeeding generations.
- Small houses.
- Financial constraints exist and hence the need for the female members to undertake money-earning activities.
- Career ambitions of individual members.
- Large family sizes affect family harmony and so small families are preferred

The modifications to the Joint Family system have mainly altered living and cooking under the same roof. However on any religious functions like naming ceremonies, engagements, threading ceremonies, marriages or any other occasion, the entire group of relatives gets together. The elders present are respected and enquired by all those present. Thus the basic family & relatives structure is very much retained, preserved as well as cherished.

A survey finding claims that well over 60% families experience strained family relations. It has been ascertained that lack of proper communication amongst the family members is the root cause for such situations and can be easily corrected. The Indian culture and traditions inhibit people from expressing their family problems or affairs even to a family counselor. Hence such services are not used even if these are available. Some senior citizens organizations have succeeded in creating an atmosphere of confidence among their members and can reach out to those who are under family stress. The counselors from amongst the members themselves then resolve the problems.

At present about 12% senior citizens are required to stay alone or with their spouses as their children are away for some reason or the other. This percentage is expected to go up to 80% by the year 2025. This increase is not considered abnormal. However since the dependency ratio will also be going up the support system will have to be strengthened. Actual experiments have proved that local senior citizens organization can playa very effective role in this matter.

The effect of generation gap is responsible for disturbing the family harmony but detailed analysis showed that this effect is more imaginary than any thing else and can be avoided by improving communication amongst the members of the family.

It is found that a large number of senior citizens choose to stay with their off springs in their houses on retirement. Till such time these senior citizens are physically mobile and useful, there are little or no problems. The trouble starts when the mobility gets restricted and they become somewhat of a liability. However by this time it may be too late to rectify or retrieve the situation easily. In such cases it was found out that circumstances like financial restrictions, physical dependence and small living space were also some of the main causes.

It was abundantly evident that misplaced sense of affection, love and confidencc had led many senior citizens to allow their sons to continue to stay with them even when the living space was inadequate and inconvenient. This, more often than not, was found to be disastrous. Such misplaced affection, or at times obligations felt on account of dependence, was found to prompt the elderly to undertake other responsibilities in the house and or looking after the grand children. In many such situations it was found to have adverse effect on the health of the elderly.

In some cases it was found that senior citizens failed to recognize that they are no more the head of the family. Lack of will to accept the change and adapt suitably, invariably led to avoidable tensions.

Social Involvement

There is a marked indifference amongst the retiring population to involve themselves in some social activities. Percentage of those cutting themselves away from the society is very large. While the cultural norms prompt a role for the elderly in the society the above trend may seriously affect social harmony. The elderly also render themselves a nonproductive entity whose dependency will gradually increase due to decline in the physical, mental as well as monetary capabilities.

A suitable awareness effort can however reverse this trend through NGO efforts as is evident in towns like Pune in urban areas and Shrirampur or Ozar in rural areas of Maharashtra. Senior Citizens' Organizations are mutually self supporting NGOs. These have come up on their own due to increased awareness' created by suitable articles appearing in the press and other media instruments. The natural instinct for socializing plays an important role. It is the social activities of these types of NGOs, which motivates senior citizens to organize themselves in convenient groups and derive number of advantages to improve the quality of life not only for their members but also for the non member senior citizens in the area of their operation. Particularly the ailing, lonely or those whose mobility is hampered are getting respite. Pune provides an ideal model to examine this effect.

8

Policies and Programmes for the Aged in India

The National Policy on Older Persons

The Directive Principles of state policy in the constitution of India enjoins the state to provide public assistance to older persons within the limits of its economic capacity. In the 1950s and 1960s, old age pension and shelter was introduced. Other programmes were introduced in later years.

In the United Nations in 1948, a draft 'Declaration on Old Age Right's was passed in Argentina. 20 years later it was again placed on the agenda of the United Nations General Assembly at the initiative of Malta, eventually leading to the advent of the World Assembly on Ageing, held that year in Vienna. It was followed in the same year by the General Assembly's adoption of the International Plan of Action on Ageing, that is commonly known as the Vienna Plan of Action (Soneja, 2000).

After the World Assembly on ageing at Vienna in 1982, an Inter-Ministerial committee was formed to create a policy on older persons in 1987-88. It gathered momentum only in the two years preceding 1999, which was the UN International year of older persons and a National Policy on Older Persons was declared in this year.

The vulnerable groups identified by the policy within older persons included widows, women in general, the poor, rural residents, the disabled and the chronically (including the mentally ill). It promises an array of state interventions – support for financial security, health care shelter and welfare, special focus on older women, protection against abuse and exploitationl special attention to rural areas, etc. It recognizes that the state cannot achieve these objectives by itself.

In Januaryt 1997, there was a pension scheme for 2.76 million people. It proposes to include all older persons under the poverty line. However, no deadlines for the completion of this programme is given, nor is there a number of persons under poverty line or the amount of funds required.

At present rates, Rs. 30 – Rs. 250 per month is being paid but various states to older persons without any income or livelihood security. It is only a token payment. There is no review and no details on increasing the amount to account for inflation or economic sustenance. Pensions for agricultural labourers, unemployment relief, etc. may also be accessed for older persons. 33% of the general populations of the aged are poor amounting to about 23 million. Many continue to work long after the age of 60 years. Their average earnings are lower than in other age groups. Therefore, the universal coverage of old age pension to the aged is beyond the capacity of the government. The same is true for other facilities.

There is no plan of action. As a result nothing has been done so far. There is also no financial memorandum attached to the policy. The policy also refers to the legal rights of parents relating to maintenance (also seen in section 125 of the Criminal Procedure Code and it refers to the Hindu Adoption and Maintenance Act, 1956). The policy is holistic in approach.

In May 1999, the Ministry notified 39-member National Council for Older persons under the Ministry of Social Justice and Empowerment to advise, provide feedback, act as a lobby and advocacy forum and deal with complaints from individuals. It has representatives from central ministries like pensions, defence, railways, communications, as well as from three state governments by rotation. A representative also exists from the National Commission for Women and the National Human Rights Commission.

Unfortunately ministries responsible for health care and nutrition, shelter, education, law, media, rural areas and labour were not represented.

The bulk of the National Council for Older Persons are experienced and well know individuals from many backgrounds like non-governmental organizations, citizens, groups, retired persons, associations, law, social welfare and security, research and midicine. A seven-member working group has also been set up within the National Council for Older Persons for more frequent meetings chaired by the4 Secretary of the Ministry. Its Secretariat, called Aadhar, is at Agewell, a voluntary organization working with elderly citizens.

It is mandated to look into individual grievances of older persons, set up a voluntary network at district level throughout the country, compile data and information relating to ageing and older persons carry on advocacy and awareness programmes.

Launched in November 1999, by February 2000 Aadhar identified 2,300 individuals in over 120 districts to work on a voluntary basis for older persons. It has to develop a method for handling grievances or complaints, or personal letters from older persons. It has received over 700 such letters from the Ministry of Social Justice and Empowerment.

A horizontal co-ordination is required between different government agencies. To do this an inter-ministerial committee had to be set up. This has yet to be done.

It classifies two-thirds of the population above 60 years as economically 'fragile'; of which half is below the poverty line and the other hyalf above the poverty line but in the lower income group. A new pension scheme is also proposed.

Poverty among older persons is due to a result of a lack of income and livelihood security during the productive years; the anti-poverty programmes are aimed at providing a wage or self-employment and not doles. Attempts at combining thrift and credit activities with anti-poverty programmes have been quite successful in recent years.

A pension scheme has been proposed for people who save Rupees five every day. By the time they reach old age, they will be above the poverty line, provided the pension assets are invested wisely. There is no data to sustain this assumption. The improvement in the legal rights of women is not referred to.

There is a high proportion of widows in the more than 60 years age group. In this age group, there is a more favourable female: male sex ratio. There are glaring differences in literacy and wages or earnings between older men and older women. There is a higher morbidity of older women as compared to older men. There is a differential access of older persons to health care based on gender.

The basic key features of the National Policy on Older Persons include an expansion of the old age pension scheme to include the private sector, a subsidized health care network with a private4 sector involvement; an increased standard tax deductions for senior citizens; legalization of the parents' right to be supported by children; regulatory authority to monitor pension funds; easy access to housing loans and special provisions in the Indian Penal code for the protection of older citizens. It also includes and Old Age Social in Income Security (OASIS) Project. Bhavishya Arogya Medclaims and Rural Group Life Insurance Schemes are also envisaged for Health Care.

Since the government cannot perform all these functions, much of these tasks have to be performed by other agencies and organizations. Voluntary or Non-Governmental Organizations (Vos or NGOs) are primary among these. Hence a look at all these is in order.

Emerging Problem of Care of the Aging

Indian social norms, values, and codes of conduct prescribed in the scriptures and sacred texts, and as they have evolved through the ages, have enjoined not only the proper care of the elderly but also assigned to them a position of honour and authority in most matters connected with the family. This status was reinforced by the importance of tradition in society, the value of knowledge of the past in solving problems of the present and the ownership and control exercised over sources of livelihood. In many communities there were socio-religious ceremonies to honour persons who attained the age of sixty. These were, perhaps, as much a reflection of the venerable attitude towards the old as also of the rather small numbers who reached that age.

The position and status of the old have, however, been seriously undermined by factors such as: changing values, growing individualism and rising aspirations for consumer goods as a result of the impact of education, urbanization, westernization and industrialization which prompt the younger generation to give primacy to themselves; less number of children due to acceptance of the small family norm and hence greater vulnerability in the matter of dependence; participation of women in employment in cities in white collar jobs, leaving the old unattended during day time and creating stress situations or prompting them to press for separate residence so that they will not be burdened with such problems; migration of the younger members to cities for alternative sources of livelihood; acute paucity of accommodation in urban areas and the exorbitant rents which act as a strong disincentive to bring old parents to live with their children; complexities of modern life and living which discount the value of traditional systems and practices and place a premium on lateral transmission of knowledge in contrast to vertical transmission from the older generation, thereby devaluing the knowledge and experience of the old; fast pace of social change which accentuates the inter-generation differences in values and life-styles; the Indian practice of total involvement of parents in their children and not developing or cultivating other interests including leisure-time pursuits which could sustain their interest and keep them occupied in their old age (religious pursuits in old age do not sustain their interests and keep them busy during their entire free time:; larger investments than in the past on the education and upbringing of children which result in less resources being available for the care of the aging and which, together with the inflationary pressures, cause disproportionately greater hardship to the old; the total economic dependency status of most old people in the absence of old age social security benefits. The status of the elderly female has been further affected due to less importance being assigned to socio-religious ceremonies in which her knowledge and advice were valued and less use of her knowledge and experience in child-rearing due to greater reliance on modern medicine, technology and information.

The above factors have undermined the status, care and protection which were provided by the joint family, the kinship group and the community—institutions and systems that are themselves undergoing a transition. There is unfortunately some degree of ambivalence in Indian society in regard to even accepting care of the elderly as an emerging social problem and of considering their social, psychological, medical and welfare needs when the family is unable to meet them or requires support to be able to discharge its obligations. This has adversely affected fact-finding, discussion and debate, which could have led to a wider recognition of the nature of the problem and its dimensions. Another outcome has been the very low priority accorded by decision-makers to the needs of this group, which has adversely affected the development of services for them.

Constitutional and Legislative Provisions

The Constitution of India recognizes the duty of the state towards the elderly. According to Article 41 "The State shall within the limits of its economic capacity and development, make effective provision for securing the right to work, to education, and to public assistance in cases of unemployment, old age, sickness and disablement and in other cases of undeserved want." This article is one of the Directive Principles of State Policy, the provisions of which are not enforceable by a court "but the principles there in laid down are nevertheless fundamental in the governance of the country and it shall be the duty of the State to apply these principles in making laws." The farmers of the Constitution did thus recognize the need for social security programmes to be supported by the State.

There are some legislative provisions for the protection of the elderly which are based on the principle that it is the family (children) which is responsible for their care. Section 125 (d) of the Criminal Procedure Code (1973) makes it incumbent for a person having sufficient means to maintain his father or mother who is unable to maintain himself or herself and on getting proof of such neglect or refusal, a first class magistrate may order such person to make a monthly allowance not exceeding Rs. 500. A recent court judgement has interpreted the provision to include daughters. Few people are perhaps aware of this position and fewer still get a court order for support, due probably to the sense of shame in seeking justice for what is viewed as essentially a family or private affair. The Hindu Adoption and Maintenance Act, 1956, too recognizes the obligation of a person to maintain his or her aged or infirm parent (Section 30(3))

Historically, legal responsibility has been assigned to children to take care of their old parents in most countries of the world. However, taking into consideration the changed contemporary scene, countries are now moving in the direction of the State providing social security benefits to the old in their own right.

Plan Policy

The five year plan documents do not show consistency in recognizing the old as a target group needing welfare services. The first and second five year plans covered only the social security measures for industrial workers. The third five year plan recognized the needs of the old without any means of livelihood and support but left it to voluntary organizations and local bodies to provide the assistance; it suggested the setting up of relief and assistance funds. An interesting consequential development was a communication from the Ministry of Labour, Government of India, to the State governments in 1963, exhorting the setting up of Social Assistance Bureaux by cive bodies and the establishment of Relief and Assistance Funds which would be administered through the Social Assistance Bureaux; some assistance was stipulated from the central government for such Funds. Nothing positive, however, emerged. The outlay of Rs. 20 million made for social assistance programmes covering the old and other categories (disabled, etc.) remained unutilized.

The fourth five year plan document (Draft Outline 1966-67, 1970-71) made a provision of Rs. 40 million for social assistance schemes for old persons unable to work, the physically handicapped and other categories. This remained unutilized in the first two years. Subsequently, the document was superseded by the fourth plan document 1969-70 to 1974-75 in which the proposal did not find a place.

The fifth five year plan (1974-75 to 1978-79) mentioned that the States should progressively endeavour to evolve a comprehensive social security system covering the needs of the aged, the handicapped and others in need of social assistance. No outlays were, however provided in the central plan. It was presumably left to the states to carry out the directives through appropriate programmes in the state plans. Progress in this direction, however, was very inadequate and was limited to running or giving grants-in-aid for old age homes as the first programme which struck the mind was institutional care in old age homes. There was general lack of awareness of the wide range of non-institutional services that can be planned and programmed for the aged.

The draft sixth plan (1978-79 to 1982-83) document makes no mention of the aging as a target group needing welfare services. The subsequent sixth plan (1980-81 to 1984-85) document which superseded this recognized the aged as a vulnerable group for whom programmes were required to be developed to meet their needs. No outlays were separately indicated in the central sector for schemes for the aged, the assumption once again being that the States could in their plans provide whatever services they felt necessary. As a fall out of the world Assembly on Aging (1982), for the first time in 1983-84, the central government started giving grant-in-aid to voluntary organizations for providing services to the elderly under a general grant-in-aid scheme. However, the State plans continued to treat this as a low priority sector.

The seventh plan (1985-86 to 1989-90) document does not recognize the aging as a target group; nor has any mention been made of their needs or services to meet those needs. However, as in the sixth plan, grants-in-aid were being given to some voluntary organizations under a general grants-in-aid scheme of the central government; in the States, too, grants were being given to voluntary organizations or old age homes run by the government, but budgetary provisions were small.

Although from the fourth plan onwards no schemes were specifically identified, or outlays indicated, for services for the aged in the plan documents, Working Groups set up from time to time by the Planning Commission and the Ministry of Social Welfare to advise on the preparation of a five year plan have advocated programmes for them—both public assistance of the nature of cash payments every month based on certain criteria, and welfare services through grants to voluntary organizations. Mention may be made in this connection of the Reports of the Task Force on Social Security for the Aged and other Handicapped Groups set up by the Planning Commission for the fifth plan (1972), the Steering Group on Development of Backward Classes and Social Welfare in the Fifth Five Year Plan (1973), the Working Group on Social Welfare in the Five Year Plan 1978-79 to 1982-83, etc., For the seventh five year plan (1985-86 to 1989-90), the Ministry of Social Welfare constituted, under the Working Group on Social Welfare, a separate sub-group on the welfare of the aged which recommended a comprehensive approach to the problems of the elderly, framing of a national policy, the extension of services for the aged in different sectors of the plan, the promotion of and support to voluntary organizations, and the utilization of the aged in national development endeavours. It also recommended a separate of grant-in-aid to voluntary organizations in the central sector plan for social welfare of services to the aged, and the setting up of a National Gerontology Centre. In regard to old age pensions to the destitute old' given by the States, it suggested rationalization and liberalization of the rate of pensions, eligibility criteria, etc. However, these recommendations were not accepted by the Planning Commission and were not reflected in the plan even through they were included in the proposals of the Ministry of Social Welfare, Government of India.

The reasons for the low priority in the plan appear to be based on the following premises.

(i) that there is no real problem of care of the elderly in India. The family and other kin members take care of the elderly and in residual cases voluntary organizations should organize institutional or non-institutional care, depending on need;

(ii) that welfare of the elderly is a non-developmental expenditure and hence funds for such programmes should come from the non-plan budget;

(iii) that investments on children, women and even the physically handicapped will develop their potential for growth and contribute to the nation's future – an objective unlikely to be met in the case of aging.

In the absence of recognition of the aged as a target group, and the identification of specific schemes for them with financial allocations, it has been difficult to find resources to attend adequately to the needs of the elderly even though there is a growing understanding and sympathy for their problems and needs.

Outside the plan framework and not directly emanating from it, a number of Committees/Working Groups constituted by the Ministry of Labour, Ministry of Finance, etc. have recognized the need to provide public assistance to the old who are without any means of support. A significant development was the decision of the Seventh Finance Commission (1978) to allow in the forecast perio0d adequate provisions to the states for social security pension (non-contributory) to the old at the rate of Rs. 60 per month to 0.1 per cent of the population (1971 census). The Commission's award allowed for an expenditure of Rs. 2641 million for the period 1979-84 in 22 states. The assumption by the Seventh Finance Commission that only 0.1 per cent of the total population is in need of old age pension because of absence of means of support was a conservative one since it implied coverage of only 1.7 per cent of the population in the age group 60+. Nevertheless, it represents a significant landmark in regard to allocation of funds in the non-plan budget. An important subsequent development has been the upward revision of the monthly rate of old age pension to Rs. 60 in a large number of states/union territories from the rate of Rs. 25 to Rs. 30 which was paid earlier; also 6 States and 3 union territories which did not have the scheme of old age pensions framed their own schemes. The Eighth Finance Commission, too, allowed devolution of resources to the states on account of the scheme of old age pensions, adopting a per capita rate of Rs. 4.6 for purposes of forecasting. An interesting aspect of the deliberations of these Committees/Working Groups was that (i) they generally confined themselves to the maintenance aspects of the old through cash subsistence; (ii) other needs and the social services to meet them were virtually ignored or very inadequately considered and (iii) the potentials of the old to contribute to national development were not considered.

Approach and Strategy

The welfare services which have developed over the years in different countries of the world in response to the needs of the aging have shown a wide variety of responses both from the government and the voluntary sector. Broadly, these have followed the following patterns:

(i) Care of the aging as the primary responsibility of the individual and his family; individual and social attitudes strongly disfavouring acceptance of public care, which was resorted to only as a last measure, with the local authorities stepping in only in cases of destitution; some countries have legislation whereby children who fail to fulfil the obligation of looking after their parents could be directed by the courts to do so (recourse to this was rarely taken by the elderly as it was considered stigmatic for the family); voluntary agencies providing limited welfare services, institutional as well as non-institutional; generally negative attitude towards non-contributory pension on the ground that it will not promote thrift and will erode family responsibility towards the aging.

(ii) Acceptance of the concept of the welfare state and of public responsibility towards dependent categories of the population including the elderly; State provision of non-contributory income maintenance measures, subject to fulfilling certain criteria of eligibility for assistance; cost sharing (as in the case of medicare), subsidies, or special programmes; change in values towards the care of the elderly and resort to public care, both institutional and non-institutional, in an increasing measure.

(iii) Emphasis on the provision of institutional care of the elderly including the development of integrated stay-in facilities covering a range of services; greater participation by the State in providing special facilities and services; widening of the range of services to the elderly and of social security benefits which are not limited to income maintenance and medical care; clientele for welfare covering both the indigent as well as those who could pay for the services.

(iv) Emphasis on non-institutional and community-based services enabling the elderly to live in their homes except where the interest and welfare of the person demanded institutional care; acceptance that the State has to ensure, through income maintenance and other measures, a certain minimum standard of well-being supplemented by the social and community services offered by the State and voluntary agencies; acceptance that the minimum standards are not necessarily based on contributions made but on need and on certain eligibility criteria based on economic status; growing recognition that physical facilities and financial security are not enough but what is more relevant and important is the care of the elderly in the community setting and their integration into community life; greater participation by the State and by the community in the organization of welfare services for the elderly, some of which show considerable innovativeness both in concept and in implementation and reflect the increasing concern of society in arriving at more satisfactory forms of care; extension of some benefits and services under statutory framework and, to that extent, conferring a right to the person subject to his fulfilling the conditions of eligibility: extension of others through adm89ninstrative and executive orders which, although they lack the force of a statute, give greater scope for flexibility, specially in regard to services in which standardization may be difficult ot achieve in the initial stages.

The current trend is to facilitate the availability and utilization of welfare services by the aging n their homes and communities. In the case of the elderly, whose physical and mental facilities have not been impaired these are designed for the individual not only as a recipient of the service but are intended also to involve him in community work to enable him to play a useful role consistent with his physical and mental capacities and his interests. Services for the aging take a variety of forms in the developed countries such as social security benefits covering income maintenance, medical care and other needs; organizing clubs, recreation and holiday programmes and excursions; centres for senior citizens; counselling services on legal, financial and other matters to protect them from exploitation; housing; referral information; subsidized transportation or special arrangements so as to facilitate mobility, accessibility, utilization of services and maintenance of links with the family, relatives, neighbours and friends; fiscal and administrative measures assigning priority to the elderly in the allocation of services; loans/assistance for making improvements in self-occupied houses or for owning houses. The participation and contribution of the elderly are sought through programmes such as foste4r grandparent programmes for socially and physically handicapped children, senior volunteer programmes which permit the utilization of their experience and sills in community work, and senior companion programmes to provide friendly companionship to the homebound aging.

For those who are home-bound and whose physical and mental faculties have become somewhat impaired or who suffer from some chronic illness, the income maintenance and other social security benefits are supplemented in the developed countries by various programmes . Services are extended to the home through help in domestic chores; friendly home-visiting by volunteers to give company and to assess the need for help; home meal services; nursing attention in the home; health aid services; substitute family care; arranging for aids and appliances for those who are disabled; day care centres; services for repair and maintenance extended at home; telephone reassurance services which provide daily contact; advice on protection against crime through adoption of precautionary measures and installation of security devices; transportation and escort services to facilitate utilization of community facilities and maintenance of links with friends, nieghbours and the community. Half-way homes for convalescence and temporary care, short duration vacation care and old age homes are also provided specially for those for whom an alternative form of care is not available or feasible. But even in old age homes, in contrast to the earlier patterns of custodial care, a wider variety of se4rvices is now available and constant efforts are being made to make them more lively and interesting places to live in.

Laws Relating to Elderly

Old age or the 'elderly' are the terms which are frequently used both in popular usage and in academic environmet. Despite the frequency with which the terms are used, their definitions are problematic. Old age is a relative concept which could be approached from biological, chronological, political and economic angles. The term usually implies some notion of the decline and deterioration in health, vitality, social usefulness and independence. Moreover, the elderly do not form a very homogenous group. Ageing experience differs from men and women, from middle class and working class, in rural and urban settings, as well as different societies.

Among the Hindus in India, a person is considered 'old' when he crosses the age of 60 years. According to the religious tenets, he is then enjoined to refrain from participating in the worldly activities and to go away to the forest to worship and perform acts of service. In industrial societies, old age corresponds with the age of retirement from active work-force. In the Federal Government set up, as prevalent in India, different States have different age demarcations for allotting old age pension and other benefits relating to the ageing years. It ranges from between 55 to 74 for men and 55 to 75 for women. People in the age group of 65 and above are often called senior citizens. The world Assembly on Ageing sponsored by the United Nations, in 1982 decided upon 60 years as the onset point of ageing.

The population of old in India was 42 million in 1981. The number of persons aged 60 and above, as well as their percentage are increasing steadily. In 1991 it crossed the mark of 55 million, representing 6.6% of the total population which is a 38.02% increase in the 60+ population during 1981-91. 76% of the elderly population live in rural India while 24% are in urban areas. In our country we have 938 women for every 1000 men, the percentage of population among women and men of the age 60+

is estimated as 7.6% to 7.1% for the year 19991-92. Among the old, women outnumber men in all parts of the world including India despite its higher mortality rate among women.

Attitude Towards the Aged

In many non-industrialised countries, there are very few mechanical gadgets like computers to store information. The long life and experience of the elderly give them a respected position in societies as store houses of knowledge. India is no exception to this outlook, except that this view is fast changing. Like in many modern nations, where problems, opportunities as well as aspirations are provided by industrialization and technological development, the elderly no longer are regarded as wiser or more knowledgeable then the rest of the population.

However, 'old' people4 are everywhere respected if they control important resources like money, land or other means of production. In an industrial society where income from work is major resource, retired people with lower income may lose the privileged status.

The environment in which the elderly people live are changing rapidly. Modern living conditions, especially in urban areas have encouraged the development of the small nuclear family as distinct from traditional joint family. Apart from specific difficulties like scarce accommodation, high cost of living, expensive medical care, with fall in income, many elderly people also a wait the grim.

9

Lonely Elders

Women's exclusive confinement to reproductive function and the attendant emphasis on nurturance have made the domain of motherhood specially vulnerable to patriarchal control. The idea of an original matriarchate conceived by Bachofen and Morgan that was taken up by Engels is no longer acceptable as historical reality. However, is Meillasoux has pointed out this myth of an original matriarchate is an acknowledgement of the power of reproductive arena and its later appropriation by the patriarchal. This appropriation has taken many different forms in different societies which display little similarities with the European model with which Bachofen had originally conceived his study of mother-right. Patriarchy, whether in its more traditional or modern form constantly tries to glorify motherhood as the most prized vocation for women.

The ideology of motherland has been held by Aryan patriarchal social system as the natural and primary destination and responsibility of women. Women's mothering has continued to be basic to women's lives and organisation of the family and fundamental to the genesis of ideology about women. Conceptualization of motherhood determine values and norms with regard to what women ought to do and offer ideal patterns of maternal behaviour and nature. Indian mythology and cultural symbols glorify women's role as mother—she is benevolent mother-goddess, the food giver but without actual control over external factors which govern the food supply to the home. The concept of motherhood demonstrates dichotomy that while on the one hand the mother is extolled in the Ancient Indian literature with every available adjectives, on the other, she is denied of basic right of determining even the fortune of her own children. Because motherhood being very much under male

Edward J. Stieglitz defines aging as the element of time in living. According to him "aging is a part of living. Aging begins with conception and terminates with death. It cannot be arrested unless we arrest life. We may retard aging or accelerate it but we cannot arrest it while life goes on, because it is essentially an element in living. Aging shows as we grow older. Aging change is rapid in youth and even more rapid prenately in the period between conception and birth" (Stieglita, Edward, J. 1962 -45).

Charles S.Becker defines aging in the broadest sense, "As those changes occurring in an individual as the result of the passage of time. These may be anatomical, physiological, psychological and even social and economic." He adds that aging consists of two simultaneous components, anabolic building up and catabolic breaking down. The first two decades of life are predominantly anabolic. In the middle years there is an essential balance between expansion and decay, while growth predominates in youth, degenerative changes which start occurring very early in life predominate in the late life span (Becker, Charles, 1959 : 9).

A problem is considered social when difficulties met by a group of people (a) result from the functioning, organization or structure of society, (b) may endanger society at large, and (c) can and should be solved through social policies and political initiative (Philibert, 1968 : 23). Aging is no doubt, a physiological phenomenon. However, the problems of the aged are mainly psychological and sociological. The origin of most of the problems of the aged are generally related to socio-cultural factors. The problem of aging has been recognized as a major social problem by sociologists all over the world. The problems of the aged in India, and for that matter in most societies of the third world, are bound to differ from the problems of the old in the western countries and other developed societies for the social institutions, cultural milieu, customs and traditions religious and community controls as also the individual and group psychology of the two differ substantially.

The social problem of the aged is moving from a covert to overt stage. As the number of aged in the population grows and as the public becomes increasingly aware of their social, economic and psychological problems, more attention is given towards them. To eliminate some of the difficulties, a new discipline known as 'Gerontology' has been developed.

According to Nathan W. Shock "Gerontology is a scientific study of the phenomenon of aging. By aging, we mean the progressive changes which take place in cell, tissue, and organ system, a total organism, or a group of organism with the passage of time. All living things change with time in both structure and function, and the changes which follow the general trend constitute aging. (Nathan W. Shock 1957 : 1). Gerontology may be defined as the scientific approach to all aspects of aging (e.g. health, sociological, economic, behavioural and environmental). Geriatrics may be defined as the branch of gerontology and medicine concerned with the health of the elderly in all its aspects: preventive, remedial and rehabilitative, while gerontology as a branch of biology treats aging as a genetically programmed process of living organisms, social gerontology is concerned with aging as (i) a contingent process relating to the social demographic structure of human groups; (ii) as an aspect of personal status in the life cycle; (iii) as the dynamic component of stratification in terms of generational membership; and (iv) as a contemporary social problem raising questions about exploitation, victimization and stigmatization. What is of central interest to sociology is not an individual's chronological age but the criteria, in term' of social expectations and cultural values, by which an individual is labeled as 'young', 'middle aged' or 'elderly' (Johnson and Williamson, 1980).

Verzer has stated that the practical purpose of gerontology is to help people lead a better life in later years (Verzer, 1969 : 94-98). Rosow mentions that scienti lil interest in the problems of old age, in terms of determining the correlates of good adjustment, began with the earliest period of modern gerontology. Since then, it has remained a matter of great concern, particularly in the western countries, due to the compelling pressures of the social problems of old age (Rosow, 1963 : 195-223). The problem is increasing in its magnitude in the western countries because the plight of the aged in these countries continues to be the same and their number is steadily increasing. The reasons for the increasing number of old people in these countries are a decline in the death rate due to advances in the medical sciences and the reduction of the birth rate, which has kept the population more or less stable. Hence, developments in the medical sciences and other technologies have contributed to increasing the life span of an individual in the world (U.N. Population Studies, No. 26, 1956).

The population of older people in the world aged 65 years and above had increased by 63 per cent over the last 20 years. According to an estilnate of the United Nations, there were approximately 260 million people in that age group in 1980 which constitutes 5.8 per cent of the world's total population. It is expected that by the year 2000 their number will be 400 million and as a percentage of the total, 6.4 (Hoshino 1982 : 11-12). According to another estimate, in 1950 there were 2000 million people over the age of 60 years, which by 2000 will number over 590 million, growing to 1100 million by 2025. They will represent approximately 13.7 per cent of the world's population (Help Age India, 1982 : 13).=live in single person households in the developed world. A small but growing percentage of the very elderly live in institutions as they need special care. Since women generally live longer than men, the percentage of women living single or in institution of special care is also consistently larger than men. The member of single person household in urban India though very small today, will increase in due course of time. One important implication of this situation is that if elderly individuals living alone have to meet their health and other needs adequately, there is a need for a whole set of domiciliary and community services to be created by the community. Many of these services are public supported though sometimes, as in England, they may be operated by voluntary agencies. Home-maker services, visiting nurses, meals on wheels, community welfare centers for the elderly are all efforts to meet the physical, social and health needs of elderly individuals living on their own. Single person households in urban areas face very serious problems in the absence of these services.

Aging—Weaker Sections

The weaker sections among the urban as well as the rural poor are also predominantly, though not exclusively, persons belonging to what are called low castes. Studies in all the countries of South Asia have confirmed the fact that low castes are the ones who are affected by concentration of landed wealth in a few hands. When it comes to the aged, those are the groups that are the most affected both by imigration and by the fact that most of them belong to the informal sector.

For poor families, the question of survival is the first priority. Voluntary retirement is a luxury old people from low income groups cannot afford, since they are compelled to continue the struggle for subsistence living in harsh environment of the informal urban sector. Nevertheless, as in upper strata of society, old people among the urban poor do change qualitatively their patterns of interaction members of the family and their immediate neighbourhood, and participate in new types of activities that are more than in conformity with their changing position in the family development cycle. As stated in the preceding section, there are several groups in the category of the aging, each group has special problems. The following few pages present the living conditions of two groups - the retired women and old women.

Who were those that Supported the old?

Almost three-fourths of the old men and women were supported by their children as shown in Table.

Table Persons Supporting the Old (Percentages)

Age year	*Spouse*	*Own children*	*Grand children*	*Other children*
Men 60 +				
Rural	7.0	75.0	6.2	11.8
Urban	6.1	78.0	6.1	9.7
Women 60 +				
Rural	11.5	73.8	6.4	8.3
Urban	11.3	72.3	6.5	9.9

Source: National Sample Survey of 1986-87 Indian in its 42nd round.

One could judge from the above table that about 10 per cent old men and women who were supported by others (who were mostly distant relations) needed help from the Government in the form of old age pension. Of course money was not all but still it could partly help the old. One has to bear

Table Living Arrangements

	Old age home	Alone	With Spouse	With own children	Grand children	Other relations	Not with relations	total
Rural India	0.68	7.31	37.00	48.57	2.37	3.81	0.25	100
Urban India	0.40	5.54	35.26	50.97	2.37	5.05	0.41	100

Source: National Sample Survey of 1986-87 Indian in its 42nd round.

in mind that a substantial percentage of children did look after their old dependents. It was not only male children but female children and the sons-in-law that looked after the old. This is worth remembering since very often the Indian parents imagine only sons as supporting them in old age.

Living Arrangements

The living arrangements of were of great significance because younger generation had to accept the old in the vicinity. It was perhaps more than just economic supporting of the old. The living arrangements of old as found in India are set out in the data below giving percentages.

In the figures given, if the spouse was there, it was given priority reporting that the old lived with their spouses. Otherwise they were reported as living with children. The percentage living alone seemed low here (6 or 7 per cent) because men and women were considered together. But if they were separated the men lived alone much more than women as seen below:

Table Living Alone

	Rural		*Urban*	
	Men	*Women*	*Men*	*Women*
All India	12.4	1.4	9.5	0.8

Source: National Sample Survey of 1986-87 Indian in its 42nd round.

It was difficult to explain why men lived alone in much larger per cent cases than women. Probably women when alone preferred to hang on somebody including children, which men did not do to the same extent. But in the advanced world it was women who were living alone more probably for three reasons. One was that they lived longer than men much more and secondly they remarried less than men after widowhood. Thirdly they could afford to live alone financially.

In the all India survey by the National Sample Survey Organizations the lonely old were asked whether they prefer to live in old age homes when alone and only one-fifth of them were prepared to consider the proposition. Further 70 per cent of them were prepared to do so only if the old if the old age home was in their present locale. One very positive side of the old in India was that they were very well integrated with their locale for its religious and social life. This no doubt created a deep attachment among them for their locale. Conditions in the advanced world probably differed, the old feeling neglected even in their own locality.

In India there were not many old age homes. The institutional living was very costly for the Indian conditions. Moreover the idea of old age home being new was not popular. Villagers especially preferred to approach their neighbours for help in old age in case of need rather than approaching the Government or other institutions.

In Indian culture people very much wanted a son to look after them in old aged. In fact it is because of this consideration that Indians were less favourable to fertility control in childbearing ages. Still 15 per cent in rural and urban India had no son in old age and 7 or 8 per cent had neither son nor daughter.

Conceptualisation of Aging

Ageing is a universal experience for everyone, with diversity in meaning and interpretation. The idea of ageing arouses a variety of emotions. While the elderly face many common difficulties their personal circumstances will be diverse and each individual will expect to be considered as unique as also his ageing experience. Their reactions to growing old and their perceptions of the phenomenon of growing old often display considerable diversity. However, within this diversity a few conceptualizations, which exhibit a degree of commonality and generally found across regions and cultures could be delineated.

Growing old has been conceptualized in terms of the joy of remembering'. This joy comes in various ways and forms. It can arise from remembering the circle of friends with whom one spent time over the years, sharing events and experiences, sharing moments of success and failure alike, even sharing the lighter moments of life through jokes and having fun. Remembering those who are alive as well as those who are no more. Remembering the happy times spent in the company of friends brings memories of the behaviour, character and disposition of each of them and the joy of having lived those moments and enjoyed them, thereby enlivening one's present state. It brings back memories of places visited or stayed and the association of friends will them. One yearns for them and their company. Their absence marks the growing distance, the passage of time and a reminder that the clock of ageing is fat ticking.

'Joy of remembering' also comes from recalling the happy moments and events shared with one's kith and kin. Remembering about the first day at school or college; about meeting for the first time a girl/boy who later becomes the spouse; the anxieties and blushes; birth of a child; about a special pat from a parent on doing well; or a spanking for some mischief done. A family photograph or album brings back vivid memories of persons, their activities, the fun and frolic, and evokes a sense of joy of remembering.

As one remembers happy memories, they are told and retold to others thereby deriving a sense of pleasure and joy. Such experiences are often narrated. The joy of remembering often overcomes the sad and bitter side of growing old.

As one grows old, the shadow of the past lengthens and the future shortens. One possible consequence is a tendency to reminisce, to put events of life in a personally meaningful order. Often efforts are made to discover special meanings in them.

Growing old is also conceptualized in terms of 'joy of pride.' This involves looking back at one's own achievements and failures. One takes pride in one's achievements as well as those associated with their kith and kin and deriving immense pleasure and joy. These achievements could come in the form of their careers, business and professions: the success of their children and grandchildren and the like. These are often recalled with a smile. Narrating these achievements, no matter how big or small, to others evokes a sense of fulfillment and a sense of pride thereby radiating a glow of life. On growing old, some elderly persons have the pride and happiness that they have squarely faced the struggles of life.

The growing gap between an individual's performance earlier and his/her 'performance today' forms a major component in the conceptualisation of growing old.

Being 'out of tune,' and 'out of times' in another way of conceptualizing the process of growing old. This applies to everything from knowledge—as it is often rendered obsolete by the ever-exploding information technology¾to dress, fashion, to music.

In old age, time can be experienced as exciting or mundane. It can be experienced as mundane if there are no meaningful activities to be engaged in, and one is still burdened with the cares of life.

In a study conducted on problems of aged some elderly persons were asked as to what it meant to them to grow old and their conceptualization of growing old. The conceptualized it in the following terms: talking of ailments, pains and aches; giving up on life; living in the past; it's a matter of age; being fearful of death becoming a burden on others; concerned with physical ageing; it's a state of mind; remembering the past; lack of interest in what one does; being cared for; grinding poverty; loss of resources; desire for independence.

According to some, to be old means to be conscious of one's ailments, to indulge in self-pity, to become passive, and to give up on life. One elderly put it, "To be old means to have given up on life, to have lost the sense of one's importance". An elderly widow expressed her notions of growing old thus, "Only when I think of my late husband then only am I reminded of the passage of time. Memories of my husband sustain me. Otherwise, I do not feel old." A sixty-eight year widow expressed thus: "The passing away of my husband about seven years ago, made me feel suddenly old." A seventy-year old man stated, "people become old when they no longer have any interest in whatever they are doing. As I feel very enthusiastic with whatever I am doing, I do not experience the feeling of being old:"

To an eighty-eight year married to old woman, growing old meant "a state mind. I am delighted in remembering my past and recall with great feeling the events of the past which have left an indelible imprint on my mind." Self-image is derived through interaction with others; it changes in response to others. The issue of self-image figures in the following notion of growing old so neatly put forth by a sixty-five year old man: "I do not feel old, but I am fully aware that others both in the family and community, consider me old. There are little things that often make me realize that I am growing old. During my recent trip to the city, acts such as offering of a seat in a bus by a young man and the conductor's act of yelling at me,. Budhau Jaldi utar (Old man, alight from the bus quickly)."

For a sixty-year woman, "Being old meant becoming a burden on others. *Mai bhagwan* se *har rozh yehi dua mangte boon* ki *mujbe utab le jab mai chal phir ruhi boon. Mai kesi paye bozb nahi banna chabati boon.* (I pray to the Lord to keep me physically and mentally fit till the end of my life, and not to become a burden on any one).

The desire for independence was articulated by a seventy-year retired professor thus: "I have enjoyed my independence all along and tenaciously fought against all odds to retain it, and would not like to compromise this at the fag end of my life. I have three children all, well educated and highly qualified. They are well settled and doing well in life. I do not have any expectations from them. Just as I value my independence, I respect theirs. My economic independence along with the positive outlook on life helps me maintain my independence. These never allow the feeling of age to overpower me. I enjoy reading novels. I watch the television mainly for news. Above all, what keeps me young at heart is my desire for the company of young people. I make conscious efforts to be in their company. They are so full of life, active and bubbling with energy. Their company keeps alive in me the urge to live an active life. My advice is keep the company of the young, and you will not grow old."

Some elderly perceived loss of friends and relations, as a sign of growing old. For them, "growing old meant having no friends and relations of their own generation left to share their memories." For a few elderly persons growing old meant "loss of resources, financial, social and cultural."

Growing old, were also conceptualized in terms of care and caring being provided. One elderly stated, "Growing old has meant more care being given by my family to me." Others conceptualized growing old in terms of absence of care. They lamented that with their children having migrated elsewhere, care was either a scarce commodity or non-existent.

One elderly conceptualized ageing in terms of it being not only an individual's problem but linked to another person in the following words: "Until a few years ago, I was both mentally and physically very active but with the onset or the chronic illness of my wife which restricted her mobility clear signs of hastening of the ageing process were visible in me. Constant presence by her side has over tinle gradually led to contraction of my professional and social contacts. Growing old is thus not an individual's problem but also closely linked to another individual's ageing process".

For another sixty-four year elderly couple, ageing meant accepting that one's children have come of age, and that it's time to gracefully hand over the domain of decision making to them both within the household and outside. He stated, "My wife and I decided to gracefully withdraw from the center-stage of decision making. Herein lies the secret of our happiness and harmony in our home. My son and daughter-in-law are both doctors and are mature to take decisions on their own. Initially, my wife and I tried to superimpose some of our decisions on them but soon realized the folly of doing so, for this often led to mild protests, simmering discontent and ill-feeling. Since our conscious withdrawal there has been peace and harmony, and our relations have become affectionate, cordial, and healthy. These days, whenever a decision is taken by the younger couple, we just ditto it."

Youth Attitudes and perception towards Elderly

In any description of the condition of the elderly in the family, the role of the youths, especially of the 3rd generation, becomes a critical factor. Not only do the old have to interact with them at several points but they also influence the nature, quantity and quality of care received by the old family member. Their attitude and behaviour towards the old member(s) of the family can be a decisive factor in the mental health of the old member(s).

The emerging trend of a large number of old men and women taking the role of "looking after grand children: gives a new dimension to this situation. (In Soodan's study, 82% of the males and 63% of the females were found to be taking up this role). Several studies indicate that the attitude of youths towards the old is not based on traditional values.

In his study of Shamirpet, Dube reported that "they (the youths) scoff at their parents, belittle the experience of elders and seem to think no end of themselves......... education shakes a person's belief in the traditional ways and creates, in turn, new desires and ambitions," (Quoted by Gangrade 1989). Damle (Ibid) found that , by and large, youths are against the authority of the old. "Sons and daughters resent the authority of parents and even defy them. The family and group orientation of parents is not reciprocated by their children."

Joni Joscph's study in Kerala (1990) indicated that while 46% of the old wanted to have interaction with the young, only 16% of the youth wanted to have interaction with the old. The young find the old not adapted enough to the changed situation. In a study of the retired people of Greater Bombay, K.G.Desai (1982) noted that the old pensioners had problem in getting along with the younger generation. 31% of the Gazetted Officers, 44% of the non-gazetted officers and 45% of the teachers expressed this difficulty. Altred D'Souza's study (1982) also showed that 55% of both men and women were of the view that their children did not show the same respect to them as they (the respondents) had shown to their parents.

The young people also were found to nurture adverse stereotyped notions about the old. Vermani and Sharma (1987) found that the urban adults (25-40 years) who had at least one old member in the household entertained the following notions bout the old: (1) "most old people spend too much time prying into the affairs of others" and in "Giving unsought advice" (63%) (2) most old people are constantly complaining about the behaviour of younger generation (81%). At the dame time (3) they make excessive demand for love and reassurance from the young people 94%. The notion that (4) most of the old people are irritable, grouchy and unpleasant was nurtured by 65% of the respondents. Education was found to make some difference only on items 1 and 4 i.e. the higher the education, the lower the proportion of responses. However on the point that it is foolish to claim that wisdom comes with old age, more educated (55%) than uneducated (45%) were found to agree. As education increased, the number of respondents entertaining this attitude also increased. Though the study has analysed the responses only in terms of one variable (education) the trend in the thinking of the adults about the old is clear. The generation gap has been widened by longer life span and deepened by the explosion in knowledge and rapid changes in the value system.

Another study (also from Haryana) reported by Kaur and others (1987) on urban samples of 200 men and 200 women also supported the presence of prejudice among the young towards the old. Thus the old people were conceived as being suspicious (79%), unfriendly (80%), difficult to adjust with (75%) should be kept away from family (75%), are a burden on the family (70%), and their presence in the family was annoying to others (63%). To be fair to the adults, they also recognised some of the plus points of the old: help others whole-heartedly (84%) share household burden (83%) and must be honoured (80%). Unlike the earlier study, this study was conducted on adults irrespective of whether they had an old kin in the family or not. However, a study conducted by Nayar (1996) in Kerala indicated more favourable attitudes. There, the children and grand-children of the old parents considered them as normal and as part of the family to be taken care of like any others.

To a question whether the old should be sent to old age homes, as many as 85% of the children (aged 25-40) and 82% of grand –children (aged 15-25) said 'no.' Even in the case of the respondents who said 'yes,' the reason was not found to be old age per se but problems of space in the house, chronic illness of the old person and heavy expenditure on him/her which the resource position of the family did not permit. Very few among the affluent respondent were found in this group.

Summing up a number of studies, Gangrade (1989) concludes that one trend visible over time consistently is that intergenerational conflict is increasing. When the young are having unfavourable attitude about the old, it cannot be assumed that the old can live peacefully in the family along with them. The point to be borne in mind is that even mature adults entertainsuch prejudice, part of which would have come from their ownexperienceand interaction with the old.

10

Life as Retiree

Problems of Retired Men

Depending upon health, financial resources and relations with family respond to their old age differently. For some, old age is a painful experience, but for others, it is time for finding new passions, or to return to the forgotten ones. Some have made helping the aged a personal crusade others are adding years to their life by joining new education programmes. Though small, a growing number of the aged is contributing their skills as consultants or by serving religious and social organizations. They are actively fighting for various demands of the elderly. These include revision of pension, concession in train fare and setting up of old age homes.

Many retired persons lose their colleagues, their work groups, teams, committees, unit or departments which usually render to them a sense of belonging, cohesiveness and support. The organizations provide goals, challenges, achievements, power, influence admiration, assurance of abilities, feedback on behaviour and encouragement. These glorious stimuli vanish almost all of a sudden, creating a void and a glut of time and a realization of the importance of the work place. There are several areas in which the effects of retirement are required to be anticipated, analysed and redressed.

Problems of the aged include loss of status and prestige, declining health and dwindling wealth, and in some cases empty nest syndrome if the children have deserted them and settled abroad. There is a growing sense of loneliness and desolation and fear of dependence and death. In case of premature retirement, the problems include the employment and marriage of their children, post-retirement socio-economic status and income, lack of social security and frustration. The retired watch with nostalgic regret the traditional values undergoing rapid and radical change, the joint family ties loosening as a result of the growth of nuclear families, the warning of the sense of the 'duties and obligations' to one's parents, the inconvenience and embarrassment arising out of the acute housing shortage and the new grammar of personal equation. As one grows older one's senses of sight, hearing, taste, smell and touch are gradually impaired, so that he becomes a part of the handicapped. Yet he needs access to public buildings (such as the post-office) place of work (whether full-time or part time), place of worship (temple/mosque/church), entertainment (theatre/cinema hall, parks and gardens, university campuses and libraries, shopping, toilets). What is even more important for senior citizens are barrier¾free homes for those with defective limbs, heart and respiratory ailments, arthritis and such other diseases which usually accompany old age. Psychological barriers for the elderly are very subtle, sometimes even his/her own children consider him/her a liability.

In urban salaried families, arrangements for aging parents to live with their married sons, has become a source of uneasiness to older people and, together with physical isolation, there corresponds a psychological alienation within the family itself because of the tension between two different value systems. Nevertheless, though the relations between married sons and their aged parents may be marked by stress, the obligations of sons towards their parents is a cultural norm and is recognized by all. Three generation families continue to live together even when the relations between parents-in-law and daughters-in-law are strained.

Unlike those employed in the informal urban sector and in rural occupations, people who retire in the organized sector have the problem of utilizing their enforced leisure time. Few people learn useful skills and develop interests outside their office job which they can use to start new careers after retirement. On the other hand, with limited economic resources and the general economic backwardness of the country where employment opportunities in the organized sector are scarce, it is difficult for old people to be involved in income generating activities. A common trend among old people, both men and women, is to spend more of their leisure time in activities connected with religion, such as temple visiting and attendance at religious discourses. In a culture in which religious influence is pervasive, religion is an important resource for the management of psychological stress, alienation and loneliness. Today, TV is the most important source of entertainment, education and spending time.

The strategies used by the old people to cope with the problems of old age, particularly psychological stress, must be seen in the broader framework of family structure, kinship group and neighbourhood ties. Those who are totally dependent are assisted by sons not staying with them, financially and in other ways. One sees great effort made by old men and women to keep in close touch with their sons who were not staying with them and, even though interaction was most intensive to with relatives but with friends in the neighbourhood, this should not be interpreted as a matter of preference but rather the acceptance of constraints such as cost of transport and long distance in maintaining contact with their sons of relatives.

In the informal urban sector old people are not guaranteed social security as are those in the organized sector who benefit from pension schemes. Thus, the welfare of old people becomes a major responsibility of the family which because of its low income, is placed under great strain to cope with additional dependents. At the same time, old people are unwilling to move to old age home for institutional care; nor are their families willing to place their aged relatives in such homes because of culturally sanctioned norms regarding the support of aged parents by their sons and also the fear of social ostracism by relatives or residents in the neighbourhood. Although this picture is changing very gradually and seeking admission for the aged in old age homes is more common these days, accommodating the aged in the family is still necessary in most of the cases.

Old age homes have not in any way solved the problems of the community. For despite difficulties, most old people would prefer to stay with their children than in an impersonal institution, are reluctant to leave own houses, their last link with the part and its treasured memories. The family, however reluctant, remains the most constant support for the old.

Views and Comments of Retired Men

The researcher met a larger number of senior citizens in Bombay in groups in the meetings of senior citizens' organizations and also individually to know the positive and negative aspects of their life and to seek their views on the measures to be taken to improve the quality of life. The elderly whom he met were typical urban aging people active in senior citizens' associations. They were in their late sixties, retired from organized sector, reasonably healthy, active and financially self-supporting. They were living with their spouses and/or with children in the cities and suburbs. All seniors knew of several others who because of poor health or lack of financial independence were leading a miserable life. Typical perceptions and comments of these seniors have been presented below:

Seniors think of old age as a time of retirement and leisure in which the major problem is to utilize one's time in a meaningful way. Although they were living with their children many felt that living together might lead to conflict in due course of time, particularly with the child's spouse. They preferred to avoid interfering in the family matters. Some of them thought that the best way out is to live in a place close by or to live in the same premise, but separately to preserve deeply rooted kinship ties.

Seniors are well aware of and sensitive to discrimination based on age. The most serious area of age discrimination related to employment and forced retirement. It is generally true that retired people, though healthy and experienced, do not get jobs on account of their age. They are not welcome in the work force. Juniors think that the retired block their promotion chances while senior executives or officers think that retired people are a nuisance. They strongly believe that senior citizens develop idiosyncrasies which affect their efficiency. Even their advice is not taken seriously.

Planning for retirement, therefore, is as important as planning for a working career or education. People should foresee the problems much in advance of the advent of retirement and plan ahead to meet the eventuality. Many till date have equated retirement with near - death because with no plan, they have lost the urge or reason to live. Even when prepared for retirement, they face an identity crises. This requires making radical role changes from worker to that of a person of leisure. Suddenly changing the habits and behaviour patterns established over lifetime is often very traumatic for elderly persons. Professionals whether self-employed or employed for wages do not think much about later life. When they are in their forties, even in fifties. They start thinking about their future just one or two years prior to retirement. Some felt that even if they had thought, they would not have altered their future. They did not have much choice. Beyond some saving or other financial planning, little thought was given to their future. The idea of a relaxed, retired lifestyle was thought about by some, particularly those who had occupied senior position in industrial and commercial establishments, had built spacious accommodation and had the children well settled in life. However, they were generally fearful of making long term plans because of the possibility of illness or death.

The seniors who were active in the programmes organized by the senior citizens' association felt that they did not consider or see themselves as elderly. They believed that they are much the same individuals whom the community has alway seen. This mental state appears to continue as long as they enjoy normal health. Seniors advise younger people to save and buy property, particularly some decent accommodation in preparation for retirement.

They also advise others/seniors to stay active and positive, not to part with their savings. Everyone who participated in the discussion felt that parting with savings is inviting troubles. The main fears of the participants were concerning the probability of death of debilitating disease, financial difficulties due to inflation or depleted pension funds, and worries about the future of their children. Seniors felt that the main factors influencing their quality of life are health, financial security, having a positive attitude, being able to have one's own housing, access to friends or family. Nearly all emphasized the importance of having a positive outlook. Staying busy, active was one good way to maintain this outlook.

Being healthy and financially independent was practically synonymous with good quality of life. Independence means being in control of one's life, making one's own decisions. One can accept help and remain independent if there is an opportunity to reciprocate. Elements of quality of life of a senior person are many. One of the best is the relaxed, unstressed lifestyle that retirement makes possible. Other positives are special benefit programmes, entertainment for seniors, having fewer financial demands, having grandchildren and separate accommodation in a joint family setting. Seniors do concede that there are negative aspects of being a senior. Forced retirement, diminished physical and mental capacity, death of friends or spouse, fear of loneliness, death, and financial insecurity due to inflation were the most commonly discussed negatives. Other negative areas related to fear of becoming a crime victim, the less caring nature of society these days, gray hair, elderly physical appearance, and being imposed upon by their children to baby sitting. Possibility of meeting with accidents while walking, fear of children sending them to old age homes, inflation are other major worries of seniors in lower income groups.

To a retired person, the problem of leisure could be the most baffling problem of all. Judged from this angle, a retired person should develop hobbies and other interests to ensure easy adjustment to life, a sense of satisfaction filling the void created by cessation of employment. Interest may be developed in helping people. Light voluntary work like arranging marriages, circulating books, collecting door to door donations for philanthropic institutions, etc., may keep a person busy both in body and mind.

The elderly who retired from industrial houses and multinational corporations felt that their companies can do a lot to maintain good relations with retired employees. By undertaking such activities, the retired people believe that the firms can be benefited a lot. They suggest companies should set up a special staff function to do just that. It could be organized along the lines of educational organizations which keep in touch with former students. The operation should do more than just make retired employees realize that they are still valued. Retiree in reciprocity can help the company as an influential pressure group. Their potential energies and their utility should be harnessed by showing concern for them by the employers by extending few token gestures such as:

Sending birthday greetings/flowers in person, rendering free tax guidance by the company's consultancy cell, rendering free legal guidance by the company's legal department, extending subsidized membership of clubs sponsored by the organization, extending invitation for functions, festivities, etc. Eligibility for use of company's holiday homes / guest houses should be explored.

What one makes of one's retired age is up to oneself. However, it is not necessarily a one-sided game. If the social attitudes and organizational attitude towards the retired are moulded in right, congenial and healthy ways, it is likely that a great deal of benefits will be derived from the retired persons.

The discussions clearly revealed that when people retire from the work force, their place in society appears completely altered. But many seniors continue to earn income, spend money on goods, donate money, act as volunteers, vote in elections and enjoy programmes on mass media and entertainment. They challenge the concept of mandatory retirement and prove that ability, rather than chronological age, should be the basis for work force participation. Their lifetime experience is more often an under-utilised resource even in the western society children. Desai and Naik have reported that in Greater Bombay, the advice of elderly was usually taken in family affairs (Desai and Naik, n.d.: 152).

Another major problem of old age is abrupt retirement from an occupation especially in the urban areas. A number of other problems are related to the problem of retirement. Donahue and Tibbitts have found that retirement is a phenomenon of modern industrial society. Previous socio-economic systems in man's history have had varying numbers of older people, but none has ever had the number or proportion of aged that obtains in the industrialized societies of the present day. More important, the older people of previous societies were not retired persons; there was no retirement role (Donahue and Tibbitts, 1960: 366). Burgess has remarked that till increasing problems of aging in an urbanized society are: difficulty in finding satisfying and substitute activities, economic security, loss of status, decreasing social participation in organizations and greater unhappiness and maladjustments, loss of health and illness (Burgess, 1951: 7-25). The status of the old is declining gradually according to information obtained by different writer, and it is creating many problems for the old. (Marula Siddaiah, 1966: 180; Kurian, 1972: 225; Jagjit Singh, 1962: 40-42; Indra Rajinder, 1963; 70; Gurdarshan Kaur, 1964:73; and Saraswati Mishra, 1976:8).

Most of the studies on old age have been conducted in the western countries. Very few such studies have been conducted in India. The paucity of such studies in India is due to the fact that interest in research in the field of gerontology has gained importance in this country only very recently.

According to Donahue, Orbach and Pollak "the first major studies of adjustment in old age were conducted by Folsom and Morgan in 1937 and Landis in 1942" (Donahue, Orbach and Pollak, 1960: 330-406). As Morgan and Folsom state "they have used the present life happiness and the index of adjustment and reported that factors like good health, freedom from liabilities, pleasant social and emotional relations with friends and family members, hobbies, work like activities and independent living in own homes are positively associated with good adjustment of recipients of old age assistance in New York" (Morgan and Folsom, 1937: 223-226). Pan and Schmidt using the Chicago Scale have also reported more or less the same type of factors as the correlates of adjustment. By the evaluation of adjustment of retired people through the measures of happiness and usefulness taken from the attitude index of the Chicago Scale prepared by Cavan et al in 1948, Burgess has found positive association between group activities and adjustment. (Pan, 1951, 379-381; and Schmidt, 1951 : 33-42). By the application of the Dejection scale and the Life Satisfaction Scale for the measurement of adjustment Streib and Thompson have found health conditions, financial conditions and pre-retirement positive attitude towards retirement as the correlates of adjustment after retirelnent (Streib and Thompson, 1957: 180-187).

Tibbitts (1960: 3-26) however, documents that while a number of studies or aging were undertaken prior to 1950, these studies tended to be inventories, surveys, and observations intended primarily to alert and aid in the solution of practical problems of welfare and health among the aged. Among social and behavioural scientists, only in psychology did an identifiable professional group emerge, specifically interested in aging as a process; this was the Division of Later Maturity and Old Age Created by the American Psychological Association in 1946. The Social Science Research Council appointed a multi disciplinary committee which eventually produced a significant report without, however, having much direct impact on established social scientific disciplines. Collections of social scientific investigators emerging at the University of Chicago and the University of Michigan in the 1940's and at the University of California and Kuke University in the 1950's laid the foundation for subsequent social scientific research. And, although conceptualization of aging as a social scientific issue in the 1940's ran far ahead of empirical research, the issues outlined in the literature of the 1940's and 1950's eventually proved to be basically sound.

At the end of the 1950's a multi-university consortium had projected three volumes which would document the scope, methods and conceptualization of studies on aging. The first of these volumes to appear was the Handbook of Aging and the Individual : Psychological and Biological Aspects, edited by James E. Birren (1959). Two additional volumes appeared shortly afterwards, the Handbook of Social Gerontology: Societal Aspects of Aging, edited by Clark Tibbitts (1960) and Aging in Western Societies, edited by E. W. Burgess (1960). These volumes constitute excellence bibliographic coverage of the studies on aging in the two decades prior to their publication. They also document the principal characteristic of these studies: a multi-disciplinary emphasis, an appropriate tension between emphasis on problems of the aged and the scientific study of aging, a distinction between age change and age difference, and a keen awareness that chronological age is a variable with limited utility in social scientific research.

The premier comparative study of aging in various societies is Leo. W. Simmon's (1945) The Role of the Aged in Primitive Societies. The general argument of this study is that the status of the aged varies among societies, the allocation of resources and honour to older persons in a given society is negatively related to the development of technology and occupational specialization, or more generally modernization.

The empirical evidence for testing propositions about the social determinants of age status remains quite limited. Palmore and Manton have presented evidence from 31 countries which challenges the prevailing conclusion; they suggest that as societies move beyond a transitional stage of rapid modernization, discrepancies between the status of the aged and the non-aged decrease, and the relative status of the aged appears to rise (Palmore and Manton, 1974:205-210).

International contacts among investigators, stimulated by the international Congress of Gerontology, have encouraged comparative cross-national research. A good example of comparative cross-national research is the six-city (Vienna, Milan, Bonn, Nijmegen, Warsaw, Chicago) study of adjustment to retirement (Havighurst, Mummichs, Neugarten and Thomas, 1969). The main objective of this study was to assess the effect of occupation, socio-cultural environment, and involvement of various social roles on life satisfaction. Social expectations about behaviour and options for involvement in late life varied by city, and these factors affected social participation. But the positive relationship between role involvement and life satisfaction suggested by most research in the United States was confirmed in each city for both occupational categories.

As far as interest in the problem of old age in India is concerned, it is only in the last few years that this problem has attracted the attention of social reformers, social scientists and the state and central governments. The need for scientific studies on old age as Saxena and Bose have stated, "is being increasingly felt these days because such information is an important prerequisite for social and economic planning" (Saxena and Bose, 1964: 33-39).

A study sponsored by the Planning Commission of the Government of India has been conducted by Desai and Naik regarding the problems of the retired people in Greater Bombay. The authors came to the conclusion that a majority of the retired persons are protected by their families. According to them respect for old age is still a value for persons our culture (Desai and Naik, n.d.: 154).

Jagjit Singh has conducted a study of the old people of a village near Chandigarh. He found that the aged heads of the families held greater authority and influence, but once his status head is lost, the effect is just the reverse. He also found that one of the most serious problems of later years is loneliness, isolation and frustration (Jagjit Singh,1962).

Victor D'Souza has concluded that the problem of older people in India has arisen because the structure of Indian society is changing fundamentally. As a result of this position and roles available to the older people have also undergone a change. He found that wherever the older persons are still in occupation of leadership position it is mainly because of their larger wealth and higher degree of education rather than their old age (Victor D'Souza, 1971: 297-304).

Kurian in his study entitled Aging in India and Canada, found that there have been many changes in the traditional position of the old in India. He also pointed out that emotional security of the old people is not given adequate consideration and that loneliness is one of the sad features of old age (Kurian, 1972:222-230).

Saraswati Mishra in her study, Social Adjustment Among Retired Government Employees of Chandigarh, has come to the conclusion that old age has started emerging as a social problem in Indian society due to the socio-cultural changes brought about by the industrial evolution. According to her, the main contributing factors for the emergence of the social problems of old age are the changing social structure, especially the family structure; individualistic values; negative attitudes of the younger generation towards the aged; and the compulsory retirement from economic activity (Saraswati Mishra, 1976: 193).

Kirpal Singh Soodan in his study Aging in India, has found that about half the aged are wholly dependent upon others. One third of the aged are still the chief bread - winners of their families. A majority of the aged had no income of their own. His analysis of the assets and liabilities of the aged showed that about a fourth of the aged had yet to meet their major responsibilities connected with the education and marriage of their children (Kirpal Singh Soodan, 1975: 66-57).

Sati, in his study, has concluded that the retired persons did not consider themselves an isolated lot as they were well integrated with the family and they did not consider themselves and liability on the family (Sati, 1972).

Bhatia's study of retired employees of an urban area of Udaipur concludes that, as a social and economic event, most of the retired people face retirement without any planning and preparation. The retirees are not very happy about the age of retirement as most of them want to continue in employment, if it is possible. Income has been stated by the retirees as their greatest deprivation after retirement (Bhatia, 1983).

In the western countries old age has been fixed at 65 years which also happens to be the age of retirement from public service. In India most government servants are required to retire at a younger age i.e. 58, and hence the problem of retirement arises much earlier (Kirpal Singh, 1982: 25).

In developing countries like India significant differences exist between rural and urban living. These differences are bound to affect the problems of the aged as well. The older people who live in the rural areas can be usefully and gainfully employed for a longer period compared to their urban counterparts who undergo retirement at a fixed age. In this sense, the rural old remain self-dependent for a longer period of time than the urban old. Similarly, in the social field there are significant differences: in the rural areas the older people may not experience a loss of status, may have more satisfying family life and may be better adjusted in society than the urban old. The health of the rural old may not be better than the urban aged because there are more facilities of hospitals and medicines in the urban areas. The rural old may not have the problem of keeping themselves busy because they remain occupied with light farming activities like grazing cattle, bringing fodder for the cattle, and supervision of farming affairs, while the old from the urban areas have a lot of free time after their retirement from government jobs and it may become difficult for them to pass the time. In rural areas it is often when a person cannot do any work that he takes voluntary retirement from the agricultural work and becomes dependent on his children. Due to the emergence of nuclear family system in urban areas, the social roles and status of the retired persons might have decreased. In this way retirement affects the aged from different backgrounds.

According to Donahue, Orbach and Pollak "retirement brings a far reaching change in a person's social role as a functioning member of the society and, as such, carries with it consequential implications of change in status" (Donahue,

Orbach and Pollak, 1960 : 330-397). As Havighurst states, "A social role is a complex pattern of behaviour which is learned by a person in response to the expectations of others" (Havighurst R. 1957: 173-179). Retirement is the creation of an economically non-productive role in modern societies which are capable of supporting large numbers of persons whose labour is not essential to the functioning of the economic order. As a process, retirement is the prescribed transition from the position of an economically non-active person in accordance with the norms through which society defines this change. The fundamental social-psychological problem of the retirement role is the lack of clarity and the ambiguity which currently characterizes it.

Retirement represents more than a change in one aspect of social life. It is a new form of social life, distinct from the previous pattern of old age, a form which has not yet achieved any specific institutional integration. Earlier societies had aged people, but they were not retired. They remained integrated with their family and kinship roles.

Today most persons working in the organized sector retire from work at a fixed age. Sometimes it is remarked that a retired person is "enjoying one's well earned rest." However, the abrupt end to meaningful activity leads to problems of biological and social aging with all the negative consequences which are termed 'ageism'. In order to discuss this problem, the United Nations convened the World Assembly on Aging in Vienna in 1982. The consensus in this World Assembly was that in the developed societies the elderly have been relegated to a dependent role by ignoring their roles as active contributors. A new approach towards aging was put forward, termed 'active aging'. Active aging implies :

Participation as opposed to passivity;
Openness as opposed to closedness;
Commitment as opposed to indifference:
Reciprocal sharing-giving and receiving;

Appropriate autonomy and solidarity-independence and dependence. respondents, 180 each from rural and urban areas. The data was collected with the help of an interview schedule and the analysis of the data and the findings of the study are presented in the Chapters to follow.

1. Learning from the Experience

Both developed and developing countries have learned several techniques and methods of taking care of the elderly from each others' experience. For example, the western countries use a number of Yogic exercises. Meditation and Taoism to improve the quality of life of the aged. Many hospitals have developed and introduced teaching and practical programmes based on such ideas. They are part of daily routine. These also include laying emphasis on the eastern technique of sense of detachment, doing one's duty without expecting rewards (desireless action), prayer and so on. They learn, practise and internalize several oriental values. Further, old people in developing countries do experience loneliness, the feeling of not being wanted and even depression. But they are socially and economically integrated in society through a set of interrelated coping mechanisms of which the most important are the family and the kin group as primary sources of structures, neighbourhood ties and social welfare services. The mechanisms which help the aged in developing countries need to be studies and if found useful efforts made to introduce them in western society.

Developing countries have learned the importance of organizing senior citizens, helping them and utilizing their services for development. The movement of senior citizens' associations in India has borrowed several ideas from the west. Some of the suggestions and recommendations made here to support the elderly are based on those which are practiced in Europe and North America. In these countries, the family, the community and the state work in a coordinated manner to help elders. Senior citizens' centres are located in different neighbourhood to help the needy. This is something which developing countries must learn and practise.

There is growing awareness among the middle and higher income groups that at some point of time in the future many retired persons and aging professionals belonging to their class would seek admission in Vrudhashrams. Such aging people like to live in well-managed pay and stay homes which can provide the comforts they have been enjoying. Building new homes with excellent sanitary and hygienic conditions in unpolluted clean environments will solve the problems of the affluent sections of society. Such homes should be built in suburbs of metropolitan cities where medical facilities are easily available. The homes must have recreational and entertainment facilities and facilities for group prayers and religious practices. Such homes should be run on commercial basis. Developing countries can learn from the experiences of developed countries in managing long-term care institutions.

Some organizations are contemplating building old age apartments and not old age homes. The difference between the two is very vital. In apartment the man or the family is free to lead his own life in any way he likes, whereas in the homes for the aged, things are controlled and regimented by the organizations conducting old age homes. Therefore, a modified idea of building apartments, on commercial basis with essential services like cleaning room, bed making, health check-up, reading room, hobby class, common recreation room etc., provided by voluntary organizations needs to be considered.

This is also an area in which India can learn from the experiences of developed countries.

Housing and Environments

It was found that housing being a major cost-oriented issue, majority preferred to postpone acquiring a house till the children completed their education or the daughters were married. This was found to have led many to tremendous hardships, because the costs are constantly rising.

In the middle class community, housing was found to be a matter of fait accompli. Most of them continue to stay in the existing houses or hire the ones that can –fit their location wise requirements and financial capacity. In the older houses, lifts being not there, any flat above first floor posed a problem for the elderly. The size of the flat is also decided on the finances rather than actual requirements. For young people who are affluent, the modern split level constructions or the duplex constructions may be a matter of status, but it spells problem for the elderly in the house.

Senior Citizens Homes' concept does not tit in the Indian culture. For most of the occupants it is a matter of humiliation and amounts to loss of face in the society. However this is not a housing problem in essence but it is a facility to be used as a stopgap arrangement till-you are capable offending for yourself. What can really provide a housing alternative is a village like suburb where senior citizens can settle down in independent living units till their end. The suburb is required to have its own hospital and other support services required for the elderly population. At least two such projects are scheduled to come up near Pune. However, it is noted with concern that, the cost of staying there could be prohibitive even for the affluent middle class population.

It was found, that some senior citizens by planning for the same, well in advance, avoided the housing problem. This awareness is steadily catching up but still it is inadequate. It would be beneficial to decide as to where to settle down as early as possible in your life.

Clean, healthy and secure environment is the equal responsibility of the society as well as that of the local government. However, various surveys and interviews indicate almost total indifference on the part of individuals to accept their role in the matter. Some success is recorded when combined efforts were put in by local social organizations. Indifference in joining these organizations by the individuals is one of the major obstacles.

Pollution, inadequate gardens, commutation hazards, insecure atmosphere created by unsocial elements, delays and indifferent attitude in administrative matters and procedures, etc., together with the indifference of the members of the society themselves are amongst the major factors affecting the welfare of the senior citizens. The situation is the result of attitudes of the society and senior citizens towards each other and needs to be resolved.

11

Urban Rural Disparity

People in rural areas continue to be engaged in rural occupations until physical incapacity prevents them from performing their occupational functions. Whether the individual is self-employed as a cultivator or an artisan or is working as a farm labourer, the chances are that he will continue to remain employed for a longer period of time in rural areas than in towns and cities. Continuity in occupational activity ensures a steady income and a sense of being autonomous and socially involved. Two of the major problems of aging namely, losing one's sense of worth and boredorn for lack of anything to do are overcome to a great extent. Continuity of occupational role and income is also important in supporting the familial authority of the male who generally continues his role - as owner of agricultural land or a small business man or even as an humble artisan - he is partially protected from the loss of a sense of authority. This continuity also strengthens the status and role of the father who has had a longer experience. The fact that slow technological change implies continuity of age old occupational processes and practices and makes long experience important factor in success.

The traditional value system according to which age is to be respected and parents are to be obeyed, is supported by religion, by the agrarian economy and by the particular institution of property in which the elderly male continues to have a share in the hereditary property of the family.

The Indian rural family is thus supportive of age, provides a formal location, a role and a status for the aged in which they are respected, are expected to guide and counsel the young. While no elder individual can escape the physical consequences of aging in terms of failing health and decreasing physical capacities, he is well supported in his social, familial status, his sense of worth and the sense of being wanted. The status of the elderly within the family seems to be affected by gender differences, by rural-urban location and by the degree of economic self-sufficiency of the elder.

Studies on the rural aged show that living conditions of the aged in poor rural areas are not very congenial. They either live with their close kin or in parental family. In spite of physical disability, they continue to work for earning their livelihood. Most of them are independent. They prefer independent living irrespective of living conditions. Among elderly persons or rural area, disengagement from work is very rare. The participation of elderly in agricultural sector is the highest. Compared to males, the female labour force participation is very low among the aged population. The physical inability, non-availability of jobs, participation in domestic chores are main reasons for less participation of aged female in active labour forces. A good number of studies have concluded that financial insecurity and social issues relating to role and status are major social problems of the elderly citizens in our country.

In the case of tribals, landless and untouchable castes which are known as scheduled castes, scheduled tribes and backward classes, living conditions are very bad. Most of them are very poor. They have little land to cultivate, therefore, depend upon other sources such as agricultural labour or marketing village products. Many of them derive little benefits from living together and tend to migrate to urban areas. The joint family system which is a typical feature of the rural sector is found mainly among the affluent and landowning families. They live together because this ensures greater economic returns to the family. They seek jobs in agriculture or village industries on the basis of their skills and labour. The nuclear family is more mobile and can respond to employment opportunities with greater flexibility. The number of land owning families is small as compared to the landless.

The Urban Scene

Joint family is disappearing fast in urban areas. Traditionally, age had a value in itself. The old were venerated because they were old. Their word was law. Even today we find in large number of families, both in rural and urban areas, the elderly advising and guiding younger members of their families. Old age is synonymous with wisdom, values and a host of positive things that are desirable in a community. Looking after the aged was considered duty and responsibility of the younger generation. In a country without social security, children are the only insurance policy for parents. Children are a necessity even when government meets expenses. Further, contraction of the joint family is one of the major factors responsible for marginalisation of seniors, complex processes like urbanization, migration of youngsters to cities and foreign countries, inflation, a visible assertion of individualism have driven a wedge between the old and the rest. Lifestyle has undergone a change. Privacy is also a fairly new need in cities. Children now want a room of their own. So in a high-pressure society, grand parents become the odd people out, the appendages.

In urban areas, even the moral authority of the community has been slackened. Today, it does not much matter what others feel or say about a person or his family. In fact in most of the localities, nuclear families are on their own and people do not know what is happening to the aged in their neighbours' house. From the reports appearing in newspapers, journals. And magazines it appears that abuse of the aged is on the increase, many more have been seeking shelter in old age, undermined homes.

Although the traditional family values of respect for the elders and acceptance of responsibility for them still persist, the changing social and economic context is raising new problems. In the traditional landowning family in the village, the elderly male had a sustained feeling of having a share in the property of the family and, therefore, of economic self-sufficiency. In the urban economy the elderly individual often loses his economic role and status altogether on his ceasing to be active in the economy. To the extent he has savings, he may still retain a sense of worth. But the sudden withdrawal from the daily activity and his dependence upon his one or other relatives, will reduce his acceptability in the family.

In western countries, it is mainly the daughters who look after the aged parents. This pattern of care of the aged by daughters is also perceptible in metropolitan cities here. Not too long ago, parents in many communities would not even drink a glass of water in their married daughter's house. But now perhaps because more women are earners too, they pass more easily from nurturing their children to nurturing their parents. What is lost in this quasi banishment of the old from center stage is not quantifiable, not quite definable. That sense of sanity, those solutions cannot come out of books or computers. Breaking with them is like removing the chains linking us to a past, to a culture, to a civilization. The old are continuity itself, heirs to a collective wisdom, with them goes whatever dignity or grace there was in the Indian family. The elderly tried to keep the family together, could keep temper under control, children took over after their death. Aging is not an obsession in India. And death itself not so final an event due to the belief in reincarnation. Death is taken in a more philosophical sense and with greater resignation, an acceptance of fate.

Several factors have under mined the status, care and protection of old people which were provided by the joint family, the kinship group and the community that are themselves undergoing change. Bose has summed up the situation very clearly when he says that the position and status of the old have however, been seriously undermined by factors such as changing values, growing individualism and rising aspirations for consumer goods as a result of the impact of education, urbanization, westernization and industrialisation which prompt the younger generation to give primacy to themselves; less number of children due to acceptance of the small family norms and hence greater vulnerability in the matter of participation of women in employment in cities in white collar jobs, leaving the old unattended during day time and creating stress situation or prompting them to press for separate residence so that they will not be burdened with such problems; migration of the younger members to cities for alternative sources of livelihood; acute paucity of accommodation in urban areas and the exorbitant rents which act as a strong disincentive to bring old parents to live with their children; complexities of modern life and living which discount the: value of traditional system and practice and place a premium on lateral transmission of knowledge in contrast to vertical transmission from the older generation, thereby devaluing the knowledge and experience of the old, fast pace of social change which accentuates the inter-generation differences in values and Iife-styles; the Indian practice of total involvement of parents in their children and not developing or cultivating other interests, including leisure time pursuits which could sustain their interest and keep them occupied in their old age religious pursuits in old age do not sustain their interests and keep them busy during their entire free time); larger investments than in the past on the education and upbringing of children which result in less resources being available for the care of the aging and which, together with the inflationary pressure, cause disproportionately greater hardship to the old; the total economic dependency status of most old people in the absence of old age social security benefits.

Living in urban areas can be comfortable for elderly persons if they are healthy, economically independent, engaged in the activities of their choice and live in large houses with sufficient space and privacy for themselves. Through their infrastructure facilities - medical, educational, recreational, religious, political and so on - these areas provide better opportunities for self-actualisation. It can be a nightmare if the elderly have indifferent health, are economically dependent, cannot be engaged in the activities in which they are interested, do not have proper accommodation, and no relatives to look after. In a city like Bombay where almost 50 per cent in one room dwellings, a senior has no place to go. In view of dwindling finances, he can not buy even the basic necessities, cannot enjoy the comforts the cities provide and cannot escape the noise and din of young children and sometimes the shrill notes of disagreement between his wife and his son or daughter-in-law.

Table : Advice Sought by Villagers

Marital Status	*Seeking advice*	*Not seeking advice*	*Total*
Never married	28.6(2)	71.4(5)	2.3(7)
Currently married	36.3(49)	63.7(86)	45.0(135)
Widowed	16.7(26)	83.3(130)	52.0(156)
Divorced/ Separated	50.0(1)	50.0(1)	0.7(2)
Total	26.0(78)	74.0(222)	100.0(300)

An overwhelming majority of the elderly in both developed and developing countries, live in families but an appreciable proportion of elderly males and females in undeveloped countries are scattered.

Deprived of the Deprived Rural Aged

As age advances, the need for security and companionship increase. the marital status of the aged people greatly influences their life styles. losing the spouse in old age brings a very hard time in the passage of one's life and the living partner has to face all the problems of old age without anybody to share or understand. Information presented below is on marital status and economical profile of sampled elderly..

The above table indicates that most of the aged (74.0%) were not sought for advices by the villagers, while 26.0 percent were sought advice. Married elderly constituted higher percentage (36.3%) among the elderly who were sought for advices by villagers currently, followed by never married (28%), widowed (16.7) and divorced and separated. But, 25% of them were approached for advices.

From the above discussion one can understand that children and villagers in modern societies undermine the real potential of the elderly by lowering their own expectations. Modernization theory also asserts that the role and status of elderly are inversely related to technological progress. Factors such as urbanization and social mobility tend to disperse families and technological changes tend to devalue the wisdom or life experience of elders, leading to a loss of status and power (Cowgill and Holnmes, 1972)

Housing for the Aging

With large intervention programmes for the control of diseases, better health care and nutrition, and improved public awareness of health problems and needs, there has been a marked increase in the longevity of human life. Old age, followed by retirement from active life, connotes loss of work and resultant earnings. This creates a number of physical, economic, social and psychological problems, particularly for people in the low income group. As housing is a basic necessity and is intimately connected with peoples well-being, it is essential to give special attention to planning, design and construction of housing for the aging, catering to their specific needs—physical, economic, socio-psychological and recreational.

Specific Needs

The specific needs of the aging in relation to housing may be classified as follows:

Physical: Being old and infirm they are unable to exert themselves very much and to climb stairs. They require support wherever the floor level is not uniform. Proper light and ventilation are required in the ——— the arrangement of furniture and fixtures should permit from movement in the house. In using a kitchen, bathroom or toilet the old often need special arrangements.

Economic: With age, the activity of man shrinks and comes to a near halt at a certain stage. In general, this has a direct relation to earnings. Therefore, if an individual is residing in a rented accommodation, house rent puts a great burden on his financial resources. Similarly, if a person is residing in his own house, the taxes that he has to pay weigh heavily on him. It may, therefore, be advisable in such cases to give tax concessions or relief. There is also a decline in the financial capacity of the aging as they are unable to work actively to earn their livelihood and, in fulfillment of their social and family responsibilities, they often spend a substantial portion of their savings, which they have accumulated during their life time.

Socio-Psychological: Aged people often suffer from a feeling of loneliness and consequently they badly need companionship and greater involvement in community life. Their housing should be so located and designed that they can make good use of their spare time and develop a sense of involvement with the community. They should be able to lead a secure life and interact with others.

Recreational: A considerable amount of leisure time is available in old age. In the designing of neighbourhoods, the recreational needs of the aging should be kept in view while allocating space for parks, community centres and recreation centres.

Measures to Mitigate Housing Problems of the Aging

Considering the problems and needs of the aging population, most of whom have meager or no income, the following measures are suggested:

(i) A subsidy in rent could be given to these people based on their income. A formula for such a subsidy will have to be devised since it involves a number of factors like income, place of residence and area occupied

(ii) Where the aged own a house, a system could be worked out for exemption from house tax. This again may have to be worked out on the basis of income, value of property and area occupied.

(iii) Community centres may be built where such people can meet, spend their time and keep themselves occupied in various activities.

(iv) Where the aged have no relations to look after them 'Homes for the Old' could be constructed where these people can stay and be looked after properly.

(v) Old homeless persons, living on pavements and slums, should be provided shelter on a priority basis.

(vi) As the vast majority of the aging rural population reside in unserviceable Kutcha houses requiring frequent repairs and maintenance, which the aged are not in a position to undertake, they should be assisted financially as well as physically to keep their houses in good condition.

(vii) When designing houses, the safety and other needs should be kept in view, specially staircases, bathrooms and other facilities, in order to prevent accidents.

Special Housing Schemes for the Aging

It is necessary to formulate special housing schemes for the aging. Some specific proposals are indicated below

Schemes for retiring government servants: Housing on ownership basis should be offered to retiring government employees on priority basis. A separate housing scheme for this purpose should be formulated with such terms and conditions as may suit the economic capacity of the aged. Special quota for retiring government employees should be earmarked in the housing schemes of public housing agencies such as State Housing Boards, Development Authorities and Improvement Trusts. Houses on subsidized rent basis should be made available to the aged who re not in a position to own houses.

Public Housing Schemes for the Aging: Special schemes should be evolved by State Housing Boards, Town Planning and Development Authorities and Improvement Trusts to enable the aged to have houses either on ownership basis or on rental basis, keeping in view the paying capacity of different sectors of the population. The savings accumulated or available with aged people such as provident Fund, Life Insurance Payments and other forms of savings could be gainfully utilized for such housing schemes.

Private Sector Participation: The Private sector should be encouraged to build houses specially designed for the aged and organize fi8nancing on concessional terms with assistance which might be made available by the Government. Banks should advance loans on reasonable terms to the aged people who desire to build houses of their own. Social, charitable and religious institutions should be encouraged to provide assistance and subsidy to build group housing accommodation for the aging. Cooperative group housing should be promoted and assisted by the government.

Special Planning and Design Considerations

Keeping in view the special needs of the aged, adequate care needs to be taken in planning, designing and construction of houses. Some important aspects relate to the following:

Entrance steps: Normally houses have raised plinths which are to be climbed by using steps. Suitable gripping arrangements should be provided at appropriate places.

Stairs: In buildings with more than one story, care should be exercised in planning, design and construction, to ensure adequate lighting; non-slippery treads; proper rails to facilitate grip; and the steps should have small raisers. Door thresholds should be avoided so that there is no obstruction at ground level in using the door.

Water Closets: The squatting type of WC is often not convenient to the old and where necessary western style WCs may be installed or sitting cum-squatting may be provided.

Installation of Fittings: Fittings and fixtures in bathroom, toilet, kitchen, bedroom and open space should be installed taking into consideration the requirements of the aged people.

Research and Development Work

Surveys, studies and research should be undertaken to identify the special needs of the aged and to devise appropriate ways and means to cater to these in the planning, design and construction of houses for them.

Socio-economic data pertaining to the aged people and their housing requirements should be collected and analysed for evolving suitable housing schemes for them.

Surveys should be undertaken to determine the existing housing situation prevailing in the country both in urban and rural areas to analyse the special needs of the aged with a view to evolving appropriate housing standards.

In developed countries attention is being given to housing for the aging and special housing schemes have been taken up to cater to their needs. Considerable research and development work have also been undertaken in planning, design and construction of houses and other types of buildings for the aged. Under the social security system, particularly in the Scandinavian countries, housing for the aging has received consideration on a priority basis.

A development Group or Task Force should be constituted in India to study various aspects of the problem of housing the aging in the context of conditions prevailing in the country, and to suggest guidelines for the formulation of appropriate housing schemes catering to the needs of various sectors of the society. The development group should assist policy-makers, engineers, architects, economists, sociologists and representatives of State housing boards, LIC, provident fund organisations, national savings organizations, and nationalized banks. It could function under the ages of the National Building Organisation.

12

Problems of Widows – Childless Widows

Widowhood (Vaidhavya)

Widowhood is a state into which young and old, newly married and long married are apt to find themselves in, often with little warning. Widowhood is a major life widowhood course marker for women in India, as elsewhere in the world. Although widowhood can happen at any stage in married life yet it commonly occurs among older women and its incidence increases with advancing age. Of the several transitions that are encountered by women during the life widowhood course, widowhood is perhaps the most traumatic. This transition carries with it potentials that disturb physical and mental well being of the widowed individuals.

In India, there were more than 33 million widows. The proportion of widows in the total female population was 8 per cent. Among women aged 60 and above, the proportion of widows is above 60 per cent (Sample Registration System, 1991). "for a Hindu woman, widowhood is considered a punishment for the crime committed by her in her previous life, hence she is looked down upon as a sinner' (Patil, 1990). If a woman survives her husband, it is believed to be the result of her Karma widowhood her sins in a previous life. In India, among the upper castes in particular, widowhood is considered as a state of social death. This social death is considered to result from the widow's alienation from reproduction and sexuality following her husband's loss and exclusion from the functioning social unit of the family. The death of a woman's husband marks the transition from wife to widow, which in turn, signals the process of displacement of the woman from a central place in the family to its margins or periphery. Widowhood is an experience or a fate into which women are apt to fall at any time after marriage.

Over the millennia, a woman's main role has been the family role and girls are socialised and trained at enabling them to till the roles of wife and mother. Their role as mother continues for a long time. They retain the position of wife and mother, regardless of their age, as long as the husbands are alive. Marital and family relationships are often proclaimed to be the primary source of social involvement, companionship, fulfillment, and ultimately, the happiness of the elderly. In the case of the elderly women, marital status is a key determinant of their well being both within the family and outside.

Once a woman ceases to be wife, she also ceases to be a 'person'; her position and status in the family becomes ambivalent, for she is neither considered to be daughter nor daughter-in-law. Becoming and being widowed can affect previously established social roles and social relations widowhood frequently involves women losing all rights to their marital home, while marriage gives them weaker rights to their natal home. the death of her husband, more than any other loss would seem likely to disorganise a woman's life more profoundly. Not only does the death of the husband bring about fundamental disruption in a woman's social environment but it also removes a key relationship in her emotional life. Loss of wife-hood means a dramatic drop in status. Brahmanical patriarchy accorded the widow a marginal status and this marginality was institutionalised. This liminal state between being socially dead being physically alive, marks the ultimate cultural outcome of the deprivation of the widow's sexuality as well as her personhood. The widow's liminal state meant that while being considered as an outsider. Thus, resulting in depriving the widow of social identify and creating a role vacuum. Widowhood is considered socially unfavourable and frequently stigmatised.

The widow's association with inauspiciousness finds mention both in the religious texts and observers of Hindu culture. For instance, in the Skandapurana (2.9.22) it said that 'a widow is the most inauspicious. Even a glance at her should be avoided, much less her touch.' The inauspiciousness is considered to result from the widow being regarded as no longer (legitimately) sexually active, and that she can no longer produce sons and can no longer be a transmitter of well-being to the family. She is certainly no longer a saubhagyavati. A life of extreme simplicity in diet and dress, and relative seclusion for the widow is advocated by the Dharmasastras.

Hindu widows are traditionally expected to observe extreme simplicity in dress and eat plain food. They are expected to don white garments (colour of purity), abstain from including spices in their diet, and lead an austere life. Widows are neither supposed to wear make up nor put on any of the sbringar (auspicious items like bangles, and sindur (Kumkum). They are also supposed to give up wearing the mangalsutra (also known as tali in some parts of the country). Among the higher castes, these expectations are still very alive. Elderly women frequently play a dominant role in running the household until the death of their husband, when they suffer a rapid and extreme decline in the their status. As widow, an elderly woman is unlikely to hold an extended household together. Loss of spouse reduces her position within the family and society.

Traditionally, women in India have depended on different men at different stages of their life-cycle. Before marriage they depend on their father and brothers, and on their husband and in-laws after marriage and after the death of the husband and in old age on sons and other male relatives. The widow is in an ambiguous position if her status has been dependent principally on her husband's rank and status. The loss of her spouse invariably results in her experiencing financial difficulties, social isolation, and loneliness. Muthayya (1995:8) observes, "The widow's reaction to the death of the spouse was mostly in terms of a sense of loss or feeling of deterioration in their livelihood and status neglect by the family, loneliness, loss of respect, added responsibilities and burden." In addition to its emotion al impact, widowhood can be a particularly disruptive experience. It may involve the loss of status, economic independence, mobility and opportunity for social interaction . That "financial and emotional problems, negative self-concept, feelings of normlessness and powerlessness, high intensity of survival needs, moderate to high physical and psychological distress were significant among the elderly widows," observed Jamuna, Ramamurti and Sudha (1995). Widowhood brings in its wake constriction of roles, restriction of social interaction, and social participation, loss of familial support from the husband's kin for the widow and loss of social status. Prakash (1994:188) observes, "widowhood weakens the kinship network from the husband's side. Loss of wife's role restricts certain social interactions". Widowhood tends to disrupt the established interpersonal and support networks that one may have come to depend on for guidance and support in many matters.

A reality of ageing is that as one grows older, there is a high likelihood of being widowed, particularly for women. Ageing process further compounds this as the elderly women are further marginalised. Jamuna (1995:8) points out, "when an elderly woman is a widow, the widowhood stigma gets added to the travails of ageing and compounds her miseries. In other words, an elder widow not only suffers because she is a widow but also because she is aged." Widow often have much of their life still before them.

Three factors appear to contribute to the long period of widowhood. First is the husband-wife age differential. Although the grooms are older than their brides in almost all societies, in India the gap between the ages of grooms and their brides in between five and seven years, in some cases, it is much more. This gap, however, varies across regions and socio-economic groups. In recent years, this gap seems to be narrowing in the urban areas, particularly among educated individuals. A high correlate of the husband-wife differential is the very young age at marriage of females. Early marriages and childhood marriages have been a common practice in India. This tradition has continued regardless of the legal minimum female age at marriage of 18. The second factor is that the probability of remarriage for widows is much less than it is for widowers. While the remarriage of widowers is encouraged, it always has been expected that a widow stays with her children and not marries after the death of her husband. Prevalence of restrictions on widow remarriage particularly among higher status groups makes the life of ageing women even more problematic. Higher life expectancy of women is another factor contributing to the situation of widows, Women constitute half of the country's population over 30 million of these are elderly, of these 58% are widows (Registrar General of India, 1981). This has a number of economic and social consequences both for the members of the immediate family and the community, today in spite of changes widows are deprived of several necessities which every human being has a right to enjoy. Being a widow, she is deprived of even ordinary comforts sometimes. She has to bear with several unnatural and irrational restrictions which in turn intensify her physical and emotional suffering. Not only in Indian culture, elderly widows in many cultures experience minority status. Apart from the problems of bereavement and subjective adaptation to widowhood, other problems such as economic dependence, social isolation, loneliness and status loss are the obstacles to which widows need to respond. The lives of elderly widows are often spent in misery.

The life of the woman whose husband died while she is alive has been made miserable by the norms of patriarchy. A widow's life is dependent upon her in-laws, parents, siblings and relatives. Whatever self-confidence she may possess, she cannot enter new social relationships and social roles.

The magnitude of widowhood in rural areas is more than five times higher than widowhood in urban areas, the main reasons for the lower rate of widowhood in urban areas would be the lower level of mortality and the possibility of a slightly higher remarriage rate may account for this. Women marry relatively early in our country and high caste Hindu widows in India are socially prohibited from re-marrying (Agarwal, 1972), while remarriages among widowed women are not frequent, the same is not true with respect to widowers. Males tend draw upon the females of younger ages for their remarriages, widowhood has been a serious problem which has socio-economic, psychological and demographic consequences.

Though widowhood marks just the transition from one marital status to another with the death of one of the partners, it draws the attention of both sociologists and demographers because of complexity of its consequences in our social set-up. The consequence of widowhood to a woman is more hazardous than to a man, since the society imposes certain do's and don'ts on the social, psychological, cultural and economic terms, she is not treated on per with other married women.

The death of a spouse is considered as perhaps the major life stress or among survivors of varying ages and diverse cultural backgrounds. As with other form of stress, this event often is accompanied by a notable decline in physical and mental health. The marital dissolution of the aged persons has a strong bearing on their socio-economic as well as mental well-being. It is frequently reported that married persons tend to enjoy higher levels of survival, mental health, use of health services, social participation and life satisfaction compared with older persons who were widowed. Added to the loss of a companion, it also leads to weakening of families, cut off from their neighborhood, loss of economic power and loss of identify. The prior roles of women are disrupted especially of their social involvements due to widowhood. This is in turn leads to isolation and loneliness which later deteriorates the health status of the widows. Further an aged widow not only suffers due to widowhood but also due to the old age problem. So these individuals constitute a special concern group in the general population due to their deprivation and social abolition.

Widowhood is likely to increase the elderly widow's economic dependency. Widows increasingly tend to rely on their sons for support emotional, economic as well as social. Dependency on the sons very often implies dependency on daughters-in-law as well. "When the son or other heir becomes the head of the family, the daughter-in-law becomes the female head of the household and the old mother-in-law is relegated to a dependent role. Tension becomes inevitable unless the mother-in-law develops a positive attitude and the daughter-in-law is an understanding person" (Pathak, 1993:298). Co-residence with married sons has its own problems. The widow must realign her relationship with other family members in the absence of her spouse. Relations with the daughter-in-law vary according to the power each holds supported by the male link. If the two women are in conflict and the son is 'modern' and takes the wife's side, the widowed mother may be in an awkward position, having to even cook her own meals separately. Pathak (1993:298) observes, "Many an old woman is caught in the middle of two trends. She grew up in a culture which did not develop husband-wife relations because, in part, spouse was still attached to his mother who ruled the household. Now in her old age she is faced with a modern daughter-in-law who is trying to replace her in her son's affections." In either case, the role transition that an older woman and her care give must negotiate is problematic, given the widespread belief that 'only a daughter can serve her parents with all her heart' (Vatuk, 1980:292). For many, this is a very difficult life-transition, with changes in daily life patterns and the risk of isolation . another disadvantage for widows, who followed their sons to the city, in addition is the strain or conflict with the daughter-in-law, was loneliness, widowhood introduces into an elderly woman's life new difficulties and leaves her to deal with them alone, except for the help she may receive from kin and friends.

Although ageing brought respect and the important role of grandmother, yet widowhood resulted in a loss of status. Widowhood and lower status among women contribute to : (1) difference in living arrangements showing neglect towards them; (2) intra-family roles and status of elderly persons devalued; and (3) family support systems for the aged is on the decline. Further, there exist differences in the status and position of (1) widow with property versus widow will no property; (2) widow with daughters.

Vlassoff (1990) studied widows in a small village in Maharashtra and found that many had either signed papers relinquishing their rights to any land in favour of the son or did not even know that they owned any land. In fact, widows were often even forced out of the house and cheated of their rights by various members of the late husband's family.

The change in status can be devastating for elderly women in the absence of sons to look after them. The problems of widowhood are multiplied in the case of widows not having adult children to look after them or happen to be childless. In fact, widowhood in the lower socio-economic groups condemns elderly women to beg for their food. In places such as Varanasi, begging and prostitution are known to be a means of widow survival. Often they are ostracised and found in pathetic conditions.

Widowhood affects different women differently. Their style and status vary not only by their location in the social system, but also by their own combination of characteristics. For those elderly widow who have been socialised into a less developed culture and lack many personal resources, the change in marital status can produce serious difficulties. For individual widows, personal resources and location are the most important factors influencing life style. Unless financially independent and either educated or very determined, the widow's fate largely depends on the attitudes of her in-laws or her natal family.

Widowhood and old age – when they co-exist – can have serious repercussions on the lives of ageing women. If "poverty" or lack of financial resources or security exist then the situation can be debilitating. There is no doubt that destitution stalks the lives of survivors. There is a consensus that women are the greatest sufferers from poverty in old age (Walker, 1990; Fenner et al. 1988). This arises from the interrelated factors of women's responsibility for domestic labour and their inferior labour market situation . Time spent looking after children means they have lower entitlement to pensions; women's earnings are generally low so that they have less income for savings and investment. The relative disadvantage of women persists across all classes. Bhatia (1995:385) points out, "The plight of widows as a particularly destitute lonesome social group has found prominent place in folk cultural and spiritual literature... In sharp contrast the vast academic literature on poverty in India has paid little attention to widows and single women as a specially poor category."

13

The Voluntary Organizations and Older Persons

There are 12 million blind elderly in India. 80% of the aged suffer from cataract-related blindness, which is treatable. About 69 million of the elderly falling in the unorganized sector today and particularly those belonging to the middle income group, the one-third below the poverty line or just above, are exposed to misery. Non-Governmental Organizations help these older persons by income generation and rehabilitation projects. There are 30 NGOs at local levels. Help Age India has 220 projects among the aged at the National level. There are 130 Day Care Centres by NGOs. There are 855 Old Age Homes in India (Soneja, 2000).

Such organizations also have to ensure that an element of ageism does not creep into their works or into the common ideas of the people at large. Ageism is "a process of systematic stereotyping and discrimination against old people because they are old... and allows younger generation to see them as different from themselves ...at times ageism becomes an expedient method by which society promotes viewpoints about the aged in order to relieve itself from responsibility toward them" (Sujaya, 2000: 20).

In 1982, CEWA listed 379 agencies working on the aged in India. Their compilation showed that more than half of these agencies were in the southern states and Maharashtra. 13 states and union territories did not have any registered voluntary organizations working for older persons. 86% provided services like day care, recreation, counseling, geriatric care (medical and psychiatric c are) and financial assistance (Shankardass, 2000).

In 1989, the Institute of Ageing at Madras in a monograph entitled 'Care for Elderly' listed 329 institutions involved in the care of the elderly. Only 4 were under the government. 189 were run by Christians, 12 by Hindus, 2 by Muslims, 117 under secular auspices and 5 'other'. 88% were old age homes, 6% provided health care and self employment opportunities and 6% provided day care facilities. 15,471 elderly were accommodated in old age homes (Shankardass, 2000).

In 1992, a handbook by the Association of Senior Citizens listed 665 organizations in India working on the welfare of the aged. These included old age homes, day care centers, pensioners' associations, institutions providing medical help, institutes devoted to research and associations of senior citizens (Shankardass, 2000).

In 1995, a directory of Old Age Homes in India published by the Research and Development Division of Helpage India referred to 354 institutions working on the aged in India. A nationwide survey and responses from 256 old age homes showed 12,702 elderly persons residing in them (Shankardass, 2000).

Between 1983-84, the government gave grants-in-aid for the welfare of the elderly for the first time. In November 1992, it was made more specific by the Eighth Five-Year Plan which gave grant-in-aid assistance to provide old age homes, day care centers, mobile medicare and non-institutional services for older persons above 60 years to voluntary organizations. In 1995, 212 old age homes, 31 mobile medicare units, a number of day-care centers set up by voluntary organizations. In 1995, 212 old age homes, 31 mobile medicare units, a number of day-care centers set up by voluntary organizations received such assessment but there was no proper monitoring or assessment (Shankardass, 2000).

There are some voluntary organizations, which have been working at an All India level to alleviate the problems related to the aged. Some of these are as follows.

1. Bharat Pensioners' Samaj

It has its headquarters in New Delhi and was established in 1960. It functions as a nodal point for pensioners belonging to central and quasi-state government organizations. It highlights the difficulties faced by the aged pensioners and other senior citizens at various forums and strives to solve the grievances of its member by negotiating with appropriate authorities. It holds periodic seminars and conferences to focus on the problems of pensioners and other elderly citizens. The Samaj helps the needy pensioners through a benevolent fund created through contributions from its well-to-do pensioner members. All pensioners are eligible to become members of the organization as per the procedure laid down by the Samaj (Shankardass, 2000).

2. Caritas India

It is a member of CARITAS International. It is the official national level organization of the Catholic Bishops Conference of India. It aims to promote care for the sick, crippled, handicapped, destitute and the aged (Shankardas, 2000).

3. The Indian Association of Retired Persons

Having its headquarters in Bombay, it is funded through membership fees, donations, grants-in-aid from the government and undertakes a variety of programmes for the welfare of retired persons. Organizes regular talks and discussions with the authorities to project the problems faced by retired persons in society. It opens its membership to all retired persons and those who are above 60 years of age. It brings out a quarterly bulletin and has a well-equipped library in Bombay. It is now working on a project for providing socio-medical and financial help to its members (Shankardass, 2000).

4. Age-care

It was initiated by Founder-Secretary N.L. Kumar as a non-political, non-profit, secular, charitable, educational, cultural and social welfare society for the care of the aged. With a current membership of 1500 volunteers, it focuses on helping older persons to lead a healthy and dignified post retirement lie. Membership is open to all physically fit persons 21 years of age and above, irrespective of caste, creed or sex. It reviews patronage from the government and is recognized by the United Nations in the U.N. Handbook of Organisations active in the field of ageing (1988 edition).

In 1981, it started organizing free geriatric health check up camps in Delhi for the urban poor. It spread networks to provide health care services to the rural poor and the elderly from the low income groups around the metropolis. By mid-1999, these camps covered 56,000 aged people above 50 years of age. It has branches at Jaipur (for Rajasthan) Shimla (for H.P.), Dehradun (for U.P.). Faridabad (for Haryana), Calcutta (for West Bengal), and Bhopal (for Madhya Pradesh). Through voluntary donations, it started a pension scheme of Rs. 100 per month to the economically weak and indigent elderly particularly from rural area intended for the needy aged 65 years and above. A disability relief fund has been created at the Age Care head office for rendering immediate financial assistance (upto a maximum limit of Rs. 500 to the needy elderly during emergencies, accidents and sudden physical disability). It set up day care centres, holds regular weekly lectures on topics of ageing and allied interests, also seminars and conferences, creates awareness about problems of older persons among school and college students, and organizes yoga and nature-cure training for the elderly. An innovative new project, day center on wheels, provides services like medical consulotations, BP check-up, spot counselling and collates information pertaining to available facilities and services for senior citizens. The organization brings out a monthly publication, Age-care News, for the general reader and celebrates Elder's Day on 18th November every year to honour senior citizens above 80 years as part of its annual day function (Shankardass, 2000).

5. The AgeWell Foundation

Formally launched on 6th April, 1999 at Delhi with support from the Ministry of Social Justice and Empowerment, it operates like a club by offering a life membership of Rs. 5000 to an individual or an elderly couple. Children, especially NRIs can sponsor their parents to the club, which is chiefly concerned with the problems of the privileged elderly otherwise lacking organized help. The services arranged for elderly range from legal assistance, financial advice, ambulance service, help with pension problems, property tax notice, wealth/income tax assessment orders, and so on. The foundation levies a fixed tariff on the subscriber, to be billed every month depending on the frequency of use. It runs an employment exchange for older persons, help line, involves elders as volunteers for social work and provides a platform to interact with other fellow senior citizens. The Agewell Foundation, while charging costs of professional services, acts as a bridge in helping members access the 'right' sources to alleviate their specific problems (Shankardass, 2000).

6. Help age India

It was set up by the Help the Aged of U.K. in 1980. M.M. Sabharwal has been the Chairman of both Help Age India and Help Age International. It started with the school education-cum-fund-raising programme as the major fund raising effort. This became the mainstay of the resource mobilization activity which includes the use of video films, audio-visuals, advertisements, sponsored events and so on (Shankardass; 2000 a).

It is the country's largest voluntary organization with 23 regional offices, getting nominal grants from the central government. It runs on charity funds collected through motivating students and youth organizations, from private and public sectors, and through selling flags and greetings cards. The primary focus is to provide financial support to other voluntary organizations in the welfare of the aged. Research and Development centers also exist, where it trains its personnel in age car. It is accredited to the U.N. and closely associated with Help the Aged, U.K. It is a founder member of Help Age International. It has so far supported 1,600 projects at a cost of Rs. 130 crores. In 1998-99, it supported 190 projects at Rs. 13 crores. Its Mobile Medicare Units (MMUs) enable older people to assume an active role in looking after their own health while encouraging others to do the same. 95 MMUs are at present servicing lakhs of older persons residing in slums, resettlement colonies and adjoining rural areas providing medicines, counselling and health care free of cost. In 1998-1999, Help Age India spent over Rs. 1 crore on the MMU project (Shankardass, 2000).

In 1998-99, just one school – Holy Angels in Chennai – collected Rs. 5.04 lakhs. Reaching out to people who believe in 'live to give' through students, direct mail appeal, the sale of greeting cards, and through students, direct mail appeal, the sale of greeting cards, and through approaching corporate houses for donations and sponsorship, they were able to raise Rs. 15.90 crores last year. Lakhs of cataract operations were conducted free. Help Age India's Adopt-A-Granny (AAG) programme is widely acclaimed for its concept. It links older people in need with sponsoring families, individuals and corporates. Under this scheme help is provided in the form of food, clothing, medical care, bedding, articles of personal use and pocket money. Last year Rs. 8.11 crores was spent on the AAG programme. It also evolved the scheme of micro credit under which some form of credit or revolving loan is provided to project participants to start income generating activities. Another is the production of vermin-compost through eco-friendly methods in Rajasthan, which is benefiting more than 100 older persons in the lower income group through each installation (Shankardass 2000(b)).

On 4th October, 1990, the President of India inaugurated the training, research and development center in New Delhi. In 1984, it served as the only voluntary organization representing the elderly on the working group appointed by the Planning Commission to prepare recommendations for the Seventh Five Year Plan. The President and former President of India are among its patrons. The governing body comprises of eminent persons from different walks of life who oversee the affairs of the set up. The Director-General looks after the overall planning and implementation of policies and programmes with the support of functional directorates at the Head office. There are 24 regional and area offices in India. It plans to have members of the governing body representing 4 metros of the country and provides greater autonomy to the regions (Shankardass, 2000 a).

The Legacy Campaign of 1995-1996 encouraged people to think about Help Age India in the wills resulting in a number of donors. In cause Related Marketing, some goods are bought and a small amount from it go to a cause like Help Age India.

The Standard Chartered Bank started a credit card scheme to link up to help Age India. The Godrej companies have also helped in this regard. The Help Age International has a network in 50 countries and its annual income was near Rs. 20 crores this year (Shankardass, 2000 a).

Formatin of a Typical Senior Citizens Organizations

A typical St. Cits. Org. takes shape when 5 to 10 people get together initially. To start with they discuss matters of mutual interest. Their number starts growing gradually and then they start inviting somebody, initially to deliver a lecture on health matter and then on other subjects of interest. Gradually they come in contact with other organizations and their activities as well as memberships increase. Word of mouth publicity about the experiences of the members attracts others and motivates them in similar activities.

When more such organizations come up the number starts steadily increasing. Already useful guidebooks are available for ensuring uniform administration of such organizations. In due course of time such organizations should get registered to enable them other privileges under the law. Formation of an apex body for such group of organizations is a need and should be encouraged. The theme should be: Getting together is a good beginning. Staying together is Progress nad working together is success!

Sphere of Activities of Senior Citizens' Organizations

Once the Sr. Cits'. Orgs. Start functioning in regular fashion their activities increase and under go changes. Initially the activities are restricted for the benefit of their respective members. In due course they undertake programmes for other Senior Citizens in the area of their operations as a social venture. This is again duly mentioned in our scriptures and as per our traditions. Our teachings say "Sharing your Knowledge,

Experience, Time and Physical Efforts with others will only enhance them and in addition will bring happiness to you". The activities could be grouped as shown in succeeding paragraphs.

Routine Activities

These activities are generally restricted for the benefit of their own members. Each member should take an oath of commitment twice a year which can read,

"I____________________member of____________, St. Cits., Org. hereby solemnly affirm that along with my responsibilities towards my family, I do recognize my Social Responsibilities and I commit that I will regularly make my time, effort and if possible material help, available for the welfare of other Senior Citizens". Their activities can include the following:-

· **Monthly Programs**: They should meet atleast twice a month for about two hours each, on pre-decided days of each month. In these meetings following programs may be included, all of which help promote quality of life for the Sr. Cits.:

1. Lectures and demonstrations on health matters.
2. Cultural programmes.
3. Expressions of views by the members
4. Philosophical discourses.
5. Discussions on other matters of interest.
6. Lectures on other subjects of interest to the elderly.
7. Light entertainment, etc.

· **Social Occasions**: Some relevant days of religious importance and other occasions can be celebrated together, which will promote interactions and help understand each other better.

· **Picnics and Outings:** These are essential activities which bring people closer and help them share their likes – dislikes, moments of happiness unhappiness and lead them to find emotional support amongst themselves.

· **Annual get- Together**: These are helpful to organize various competitions as well as opportunities to display individual talents and promote confidence amongst members.

· **Monthly Bulletins**: This activity helps in many ways. Apart from informing the details of the programs to be help in the coming month and brief on programs help in the previous month. They also can convey a lot of useful information to the members and give them a chance to write articles and express their views. There are many things one may wish to acquire while some want to dispose off some items. This bulletin can be ideal medium to reach each other in such matters.

Socially Oriented Programmes

These programmes are meant for everybody, especially for all the elderly residing in the area of operation of the organization and in particular for those whose mobility is hampered and are restricted to their homes or even to their beds. These programmes also provide a platform for interaction between various age groups of the society. These activities could be listed as under'.

· **Let us Help Each Other**: Under this plan each member is expected to identify and elderly person, residing close to his own house, whose mobility is hampered. The member gives half an hour every week to such elderly. Giving just company, enquiring about their health, reading for them, running small errands for them etc. can go a long way making such people feel that they are still a part of the society.

· **Counselling Centers**: Maintaining family harmony, financial management, housing needs, making of wills, legal matters and a number of other domestic problems can be solved if a trust-worthy counselors are available from amongst the members. Suitably qualified members themselves, to a great advantage, run such centers. Some members can be specially trained for this purpose.

Day Care Centeres for the Elderly: A place where the elderly can spend the time of the day, indulging in the activity of their choice, just like a crèche for children, Particularly useful for the elderly whose movements are restricted, who can be dropped in the center by their relatives. For those with smaller living spaces and those where all the young in the house are busy, these can be a very useful facility. The elderly can get the company of their age group and the younger generations get the necessary freedom. Each Sr. Cits. Org. can run it on voluntary basis provided they have premises for this purpose. Local governments can help out in this matter. The facilities at the centers can be increased in phases. These are better suited than the Sr. Cits. Homes and also help to preserve family system.

· **Medical Equipment Centyers for Patients**: These can be provided at the selected hospitals and medical stores in the area of operation. The medical equipments required for short durations during illness can be made available at short durations during illness can be made available at negligible rents. This can help many to even avoid hospitalization. Crutches, walkers, water/air beds, portable oxygen equipment etc., can be made available under this scheme.

· **Volunteer Support Groups**: This group of member volunteers can identify those elderly who are staying alone or with their spouses in the area of their operation and offer them support, round the clock, to deal with any eventualities they are not in a position to handle. For this purpose a proper record can be maintained and contact phone numbers can be exchanged.

· **Consumer Awareness Center**: Sr. Cits. Living in the area of operations at times can be victims of losing their dues on account of ignorance. Such center run by volunteer members can bring relief in such matters.

· **Senior Citizens' Forum**: This activity can provide a suitable platform for interaction between various age groups of the society, discussions on matters of concern, of social interest, and on many other aspects affecting the welfare of the senior citizens by organizing open dialogue with the local government authorities.

· **Money Earning Activities**: These include cooperative ventures like Grocery Shop etc., Technical Consultancy Services, Part time Work Services, Holistic Therapy centers run by trained members, Publication of Information brochures / maps etc.

· **Adoption of Slum Areas**: A slum area in the area of operation can be adopted to organize support services for the Sr. Cits. Residing there. This can go a long way in ensuring social harmony in addition to bringing relief to the Sr. Cits.

· **Participation in Governance** : The organization can give a helping hand top the local authorities including the police department. Some of those who cannot put in physical effort can take up pen and express their appreciations as well as concerns through the medium of news papers, magazines and with government authorities. Some can organize peaceful demonstrations to highlight concerns of public interest.

· **Publication of Annual Special Issues**: An annual special issue can include information on vital issues for the elderly. Such issues can be retained for reference. They can cover subjects like hobbies, health, local who's who, area, map and such material can be of use for the general public as well. This can also be a source for finance.

· **Promote Community Living**: To overcome housing problems as well as financial strains for those who are staying alone or with their spouses, one way co8uld be to share an apartment by like-minded people. Two or more couples can pool their resources and can stay together. This can also help to support each other physically and mentally. Sr. Cits'. Orgs. Can offer an opportunity for the like minded people to come in close contact with each other.

Special Programs on Occasions

These programs can be undertaken from time to time for the benefit of the members as well as others concerned and may include following.

· **Health Camps**: These can be organized from time to time for carrying out medical checkups; specific therapy Routines; eye and other operations which can be conducted as OPD procedures; teaching yoga, meditation and for philosophical discourses and similar other activities.

· **Workshops:** These can include imparting training of Sr. Cit. Volunteers in counseling techniques; holistic therapy techniques like acupressure & reiki etc.; computer training; Yoga; pranayam; meditation etc.

· **Seminars and Conferences**: Organizing such activities helps in many ways to help improve the quality of life as one learns about new ideas, methods and procedures. The subjects chosen should include health, family integration, social harmony, culture and knowledge. It is essential to circulate technical reports based on the seminars and conferences conducted.

· **Research Projects on Gerontology and Geriatrics**: Need based surveys to generate data base and identify critical areas for taking up suitable programs to improve the quality of life are essential. Apex bodies having suitable advisory capacity like Academy of Sr. Cits. Or Center for Gerontology and Elderly Medicine can be of great help to undertake such studies.

· **Provision of Human Resource**: When ever need arises volunteers or technically qualified man power can be made available to assist scholars in such projects.

· **Awareness Drives**: From time to time awareness and promotion drives can be undertaken to promote the cause of Sr. Cits. For this purpose use of all media instruments can be made. It is also necessary to make the following generation aware of the need to plan for retirement.

Apex Bodies of Senior Citizens' Organizations

It is essential to have apex bodies of Sr. Cits. Orgs. For ensuring coordination of activities and to act as a link between the government at respective levels and the Sr. Cits in particular. These apex bodies should be ideally at city/town, district, state and national levels. These bodies can also be considered as pressure groups on behalf of the Sr. Cits. Their activities can be listed as under which can be suitably modified to suit the level of operation as the occasion arises:

- Create unity amongst Sr. Cits. Orgs. By organizing suitable programs for exchange of experience, sharing of resources, etc.
- Coordination of activities of all such organizations.
- Undertake research projects in geriatrics and gerontology.
- Suggest subjects for study circles, lectures, seminars, etc.
- Generate and publish literature promoting the cause of the elderly.
- Establish communication with dealing offices at all levels of governance and project and pursue points concerning the Sr. Cits.
- Establishing links with the Industry and Commerce establishments to examine the opportunities for second careers for the needy Sr. Cits. as well as explore help in establishing day care centers for the elderly in selected areas.
- Create shadow cabinets and help the governance by making productive suggestions at respective levels particularly in implementation of the "Action Plan on Ageing".

How can the Government Help Mobilization Strategies and Actions at Government Levels

In view of our financial constraints some drastic steps may have to be taken. If these steps are in conformity with our cultural and philosophical teachings then it may not be difficult ot be accepted by the masses at large. The initiation of mobilization at the middle class urban population level, who being educated and comparatively more amenable to reason has a better chance of success. It may not be then difficult to modify the model to suit rural and other conditions of the elderly population. Keeping these aspects in view some strategies and actions are suggested in succeeding paragraphs.

Towards Active Ageing

In view of the global dimension of the aged, the United Nations organized the World Assembly on Ageing in Vienna in 1982 as a forum to launch an international action programme aimed at guaranteeing economic and social security to older persons as well as providing them with opportunities to contribute to national development. In the documents circulated during the conference and in the recommendations entitled 'Vienna International Plan of Action on Ageing' (United Nations, 1982). The World Assembly on ageing among other measures sponsored the idea of active ageing as an important strategy for the adjustment of the ageing in modern societies (V.D'Souza: 1993,54(13),333-44). The Vienna International Plan of Action on Ageing lays great stress on creating conditions which enable the ageing to live with their close relatives as long as possible. Article 17 of the Vienna International Plan of Action points out humanitarian issues related to specific needs as health and nutrition, housing and environment, family, social welfare, income, security, employment and education of the elderly. From the development point of view, society should guarantee to all persons regardless to age, the right to belong participate and contribute. The recognition of inter-dependence between the development of ageing and that of society would make it evident that the social resources invested in the betterment of ageing instead of a drain on the economy are on the contrary a productive investment having both tangible and intangible benefits. (Indian Journal of Social Work, 1993,54 (13), 333-44).

Active ageing accordingly deals with the way in which ageing can contribute to development, focusing on the welfare of the aged themselves. Countering the disengagement theory, the active ageing has some similarity with the 'Activity Theory' but with a wider connotation. Unlike the activity theory active ageing implies attainment of certain objectives on the part of the elderly such as economic security, sense of purpose and meaning in life and integration in the community and society. Active ageing embraces a very broad perspective including the inter-relationship between the humanitarian and development needs of the elderly and those as the society. (United Nations Activities >United Nations Logo for the International Year of Older Persons= Bulletin on Ageing, 1998, No.1, P.11).

The United Nation's Official logo for the year of older persons: I YOP 1999 (1-10-1998 to 31-12-1999) is meant to represent vitality, diversity and interdependence as well as movement and progression. Vitality refers to the increased ability as mind and spirit made possible by healthy life styles as people age. The combination of vitality and diversity is seen as heralding both >a new age for old age' and the reality of > old age in a new age= This draws attention to the independence and interdependence of the generations, which create a dynamic and reciprocal exchange and caring. This ideal of reciprocity is reflected in the theme for the year 'towards a society for all ages' (United Nations, New York `1997, Department for Policy Co-ordination and Sustainable Development, Older Persons in Countries with Economies in Transition, Designing a Policy Response, 126-31).

Social Welfare

At present there appear to be no organized social care systems for the welfare of the senior citizens in India. There being no social security projects nor any s6ystem to collect any funds for the purpose the elderly population have been left to fend for themselves. This situation is likely to continue for the time to come.

Those senior citizens who are staying alone present soft targets for the unscrupulous antisocial elements to fob and even to murder. It was found that those living in such conditions are leading a life of insecurity, uncertainty and constant scare.

It was found that in the absence of any organized social care, local senior citizens organizations and some NGOs. Are trying to create and extend such facilities-within the area or their operations. Some of these are on voluntary basis while some are against nominal payments. Amongst the praise- worthy ventures are as stated below :

- Day Care Centers for the senior citizens.
- Alternate Therapy Clinics run by senior citizens themselves. Reiki, Acupressure.
- Water Therapy etc., are popular.
- Let us Help Each Other's projects. In this each member of a senior citizens staying around his own house, whose movements are restricted and visit them at least once a week. Just giving company, reading out something, running small errands for them, accompanying them to doctors, etc., has been found to bring relief not only to the elderly but also to the other members of the family
- Financial management workshops.
- "Sewa Mandals". These are formed by volunteer senior citizens, who offer 24 hour emergency support to those senior citizens who are staying alone. They also extend help to them in acquiring help like carpenter, electrician and mason etc. and run other errands for them.
- Health checkup camps.

Many other activities are also organized to help senior citizens to improve their quality of life.

The surveys have shown that majority of people want to create social platforms like the senior citizens organizations. In 1992 there were ony 7 senior citizens organizations in Pune, which figure has touched 78 as on 02 June 2002. They represent about 15,.000 senior citizens in Pune. This trend is a healthy sign of social awareness and this number is going up every month.

The findings regarding the senior citizens homes (Old age homes) in Pune indicate that not all these are popular and are being used under exasperation if not duress. The majority of the occupants are there because of family disharmony, financial constraints or living space problems. The growth of these establishments in and around Pune has been limited from about 11 in 1992 to about 32 as on 02 June 2002. Most of them are under-subscribed. In those based on total charity, the facilities are totally inadequate. Some of the State Government subsidized establishments as well as those run by recognized foundations were founds to be popular. Those run on commercial basis were found to be grossly under subscribed and costly. One aspect common to all, almost without exception, is the fact, that most of these establishments do NOT entertain ailing clients. It was observed that the occupants of these establishments were living under constant pressure all the time with a worry as to where to go during illness or after the physical dependence increases.

Index

A

Age
Classes, 34
Stratification Model, 152
Aged in India, 76
Policies and Programme for-, 159
Aged Population, 111, 144, 145, 216
In India, 57, 60
Ageing
Population, 103, 108
Process, 93, 97, 98, 102
Restructuring of-, 102
Sociology, 34
Specific Needs, 222
Economic, 222
Physical, 222
Recreational, 223
Socio-Psychological, 222
Agricultural Labourers, 49, 216
Agro-Based Technologies, 37
Alienation and Loneliness, 40
American
Culture, 77
Psychological Association, 204
Andhra Pradesh—Punjab, 37
Anti-Poverty Programme, 162
Aryan Patriarchal Social System, 177
Association of Senior Citizens, 238
Ayurvedic Medicines, 102

B

Backward Classes, 216
Below Poverty Line, 237
Brahmans of
Karnataka, 22
Tamil Nadu, 22

C

Cancer, 51
Caste Groups, 32, 43
Childhood Marriages, 231
China, 30, 31, 117
Chronic Illness, 51
Churchill, 128
Citizen Development Society, 55

Columbia, 31
Community (ies), Agrarian, 110
  Mental Health, 99, 100
  Problems, 82, 87
  Program, 81
  Hindu, 44
  Indian Rural-, 110
  Rural, 110
Counseling
  Centres, 246
  Services, 146, 172
Cultural Agency, 74
Cultural—Regional Diversity, 23
Customs, 79
Customs and Traditions, 179

D

Dalits, 35
Day Care Centres, 55, 131, 237, 238, 247, 253
Declaration on Old Age Rights, 159
Degradation in Socio-Economic Status, 60
Dejection Scale, 204
Demographic Changes, 140
Developed Countries, 24, 30, 65, 221
Developing Countries, 24, 30-32, 50, 65, 69, 81, 83, 125, 126, 129, 135, 142, 208, 209, 221
Development Changes, 36
Dietary Measures, 89
Directive Principles of State Policy, 58, 159, 165
Disability, 25
Diseases,
  Chronic, 93
  Communicable
    Degeneration, 50
  Infection, 50
  Respiratory, 50
Drug Addicts, 81

E

Economic
  Backwardness, 197
  Capital, 121
  Dependency, 220, 232
  Dependency Status, 164
  Development, 58
  Order, 209
  Resources, 197
Economies, Agricultural and Handicaps, 111
Economy, 218
  Agrarian, 216
Education, 32, 102, 163
  Adult, 81
  Programme, 195
  Sex, 81
Eighth Finance Commission, 170
Elderly
  Needs, 139

Population, 122, 124
Widows, 232, 233
Elderly, Social/Health Perspective, 69
Emancipation of Women, 141
Employees Provident Fund and Misc. Pension Act, 59
Environmental Protection Activities, 105

F

Family
Planning, 81
Support System, 103, 234
System, 155
Female
Labour Force, 216
Workforce Participation, 49
Fertility
And Mortality, 69, 70
Control, 185
Five Year Action Plan, 2000-2005, 129
Five Year Plan (5th), 167, 168
Five Year Plan (6th), 167
Five Year Plan (7th), 167
Five Year Plan (8th), 238
Forest Resources, 43
France, 31
Franklin, Benjamin, 128
Free Insurance, 105, 127
Functionalist and Monolithic, 84
Fundamental Rights, 58

G

Geriatric Services, 127
Gerontology, 17, 26-28, 144, 179
History, 28
Social, 26, 28, 36, 82, 85, 205
Globalization, 143-145
Globalization and Aged, 143

H

Health
Care Shelter, 160
Education, 85, 86
Insurance Scheme, 85, 88
Myth, 150
Programmes, 88
Health/Medical Care Services, 84
Help Age India, 47
Hemingway, Ernest, 128
Hindu
Adoption and Maintenance Act, 165
Life Stages, 74
Widow, 229
Homo Sapiens, 99
Hospitals and Medicines, 205
Housing Problems for Ageing, 223

I

Important Voluntary Organizations, 239

Age Care, 240
Age Well Foundation, 241
Bharat Pensioners Samaj, 239
Caritas India, 239
Help Age India, 242, 244
Indian Ass of Retired Persons, 239
Senior Citizens Organization, 244
Functions, 245-250
Income
Generating Terms, 19
Generation, 57, 237
Tax, 127
India and Nepal, 44
Indian
Cultural Heritage, 34
Culture, 153, 156, 212, 232
Elderly, 62
Gerontological Association, (IGA), 32
Joint Family, 32
Mythology, 178
Philosophy, 106
Social Organization, 77
Social Structure, 80
Indonesia, 18, 30
Industrial
Advancement, 66
Categories, 49
Evolution, 207
Industrialization, 32, 71, 112, 163, 175
Industrialized Nations, 18
Information
Revolution, 102
Technology, 74
Infrastructural Facilities, 220
Insurance, 20
International Plan of Action, 159
Inter-University Training Institute, 28

J

Jammu and Kashmir, 47
Japan, 31
Joint Family (ies), 35, 76, 196, 201
Joint Family System, 109-112, 155, 217

L

Labour Market, 19
Landless Workers in Agriculture, 141
Legal
Protection, 85
Protection Measures, 86
Legislation and Policy Measures, 57, 58, 60
Life Cycle, 26
Life Expectancy, 21, 22, 31, 57, 125
Life Expectancy of Females, 48

Women, 231
Life
Satisfaction Scale, 204
Span, 21
Literacy, 105, 162
Adult, 127

M

Mahabharata and Bhagawatgita, 107
Manusmriti, 153
Marital Counseling, 81
Marriage Age, 231
Medical
Aid, 82
Care Problems, 83
Problems, 50
Meditation, 54, 209
Migration, 217
Ministry of
Agriculture, 37
Finance, 169
Labour, 169
Social Justice, 161
Social Welfare, 168
Mobile
Geriatric Care Centres, 88
Hospital Vans, 102
Medicare Units, 238, 239
Modernization, 64, 73, 112
Modernization Theory, 221
Mohammad Prophet, 18
Multinational Corporations, 201

N

National
Institute of Agricultural Extension Management, 37
Agricultural Technology Project (NATP), 37
Commission for Human Rights, (NHRC), 161
Commission for Women, 161
Commission,129
Council for Older Persons, 59
Old Age Pension Scheme, 59
Policy for Older Persons, 161, 162
Policy on Elderly, 129
Policy on Older Persons, 59, 160
Social Assistance Programme, 59
Nazis, 128
Non-Governmental
Organization (NGO), 42, 132, 134, 146, 155, 157, 161, 163, 237
Agencies, 100
Infrastructure, 133
Nuclear
Families, 196
Family, 217
Family System, 109, 110

Nursing Homes, 30, 47, 105, 198, 211, 237, 238, 254

O

Old Age
- Pension (OAP), 19, 159, 160, 170
- Social Security (OASS), Project, 162, 220

P

Panchayats, 59
Patriarchal Social Structure, 29
Pension
- For Agricultural Labour, 160
- Scheme, 160, 162, 198

Pensioners, 141
Pensions, 20
Philanthropic Institutions, 201
Planning
- Economic and Social-, 58
- Financial, 200
- For Retirement, 199
- Social, 225
- Socio-Economic, 206

Plastic Money, 74
Pollution, 213
Population, 29, 30, 31, 33-35, 55, 65
- Aged, 69
- Ageing, 64-66, 69, 70
- Elderly, 23, 32, 47, 48
- Female, 48
- Growth Rate, 69
- Japan, 29
- Old Aged, 34
- Older, 149
- Rural, 73
- World, 30

Post-Retirement Life, 103
Primary Health Centres, 86
Primitive Tribes, 21
Problems
- Financial, 119
- Health, 119
- Of Aged, 196

Psychological Social, 146
Psychological, 121
- Social, 207, 222
- Socio-Psychological, 120

Psychological
- Alienation, 196
- Stress, 197

Public Housing Scheme for-, 224
Pythagoras 18, 39

Q

Quality of Community Life, (QCL), 100

R

Raman, CV, 128
Re-Employment, 100

Rehabilitation Projects, 237
Relief and Assistance Fund, 166
Religious
  Activities, 54
  Groups, 43
Retired Generations, 103
Retirement, 19, 20, 24, 28, 29, 71, 75, 103, 104, 107, 113, 115, 119, 124, 149, 153, 196, 199, 201, 202, 208, 209, 222
  Age, 57
  Benefits, 58
  Compulsory, 111
  Voluntary, 181
Role
  Conflict, 64
  Expectation, 64
  Isolation, 63
Rural
  Aged, 216
  Group Life Insurance Scheme, 162
  India, 21

S

SAARC Nations Consultations on Ageing, 129
Scheduled Castes/Tribes, 216
Schemes for Retiring Government Servants, 224
Sector,
  Rural Agricultural, 20
  Urban Informal, 20
Security,
  Economic, 59, 252
  Financial, 59, 160
Social, 53, 57, 70, 71, 141, 145, 161, 164, 168, 172, 173, 196
Self-Help Groups (SHGs), 61
Senile Degradation, 29
Senior Citizens (SC), 43, 44, 52, 57, 59, 125-138, 152, 154-157, 172, 198, 199, 209, 211, 213, 247
  Association, 140, 198, 200
  Centres, 52, 105, 126, 211
  Employment Opportunities, 146
  Forum, 247
  Homes, 155, 212
  Movement, 133
  Organization, 156, 157, 198, 254
Sensory-Motor
  Adjustment, 97
  Conditions, 97
Service Centre for the Ageing, 54
Seventh Finance Commission, 169
SEWA Mandals, 253
Sexual Myth, 152
Shashtya-badi Purthic, Ceremony, 22
Shaw, George Bernard, 128
Skandpurana, 229
Social
  Adjustment, 100

Adjustment in Old Age, 28
Ageing, 36
And Commercial Institutions, 127
And Cultural Events, 22
Assistance Bureaux, 166
Capital, 122
Change, 19, 71
Environment, 23
Network, 76, 77, 80
Order, 44
Participation, 57
Policies, 178
Problems of Old Age, 25, 180
Revolution, 133
Rights, 146
Security Scheme of Pension, 53
System, 76
System Institutes, 36
Workers, 80, 146
Socialization, 114
Socially Oriented Programme, 132
Society (ies), 18, 19, 21, 22, 26, 35, 40-43, 54, 72, 74, 75, 80, 82, 101, 113, 115-117, 121, 122, 126, 127, 131, 132, 134, 142, 151, 152, 163, 182, 217, 232, 252
Agricultural, 112
American, 77
Developed, 179
Gerontological, 28
Hindu, 44
Indian, 22, 32, 33, 40, 45, 78, 110, 112, 164, 207
Industrial, 110, 112, 174
Industrialized, 72, 111
Industrialized Modern, 70, 202
Modern, 24, 122, 123
Oriented Programme, 246
Pre-Industrial, 107, 111, 112, 117
Primitive, 205
Western, 110, 205
Socio-Economic
Development, 21
Groups, 235
System, 202
South East Asian Region
Countries, 31, 32
Bangladesh, 31
India, 31
Indonesia, 31
Maldives, 31
Myanmar, 31
Nepal, 31
Sri Lanka, 31
Thailand, 31
Special Housing Schemes, 224
Sweden, 31

T

Tagore, Rabindranath, 128
Taoism, 209

Technical Group on Population, 70
Technological Development, 35
Technology, Industrial, 112
Thailand, 31
Theory of Karma, 127
Trade and Commerce, 49
Traditional
    Chinese Culture, 117
    Value System, 215
Traditionalism, 33
Training For Income Generation, 54
Tribal Belts, 43

U

Unemployment Relief, 160
United Nations, 30, 99, 144, 159, 174, 180, 209, 251, 252
    International Year of Older Persons, 160, 252
University of
    California, 204
    Chicago, 204
Urbanization, 32, 64, 73, 112, 163, 217, 219
    And Industrialization, 140
Urinary Tract Infections, 50

V

Vanaprasthasrama, 107
Vanashram Dharma, 44
Vedic Heritage, 44
Vedic Seers, 44
Vienna International Plan of Action on Ageing, 251
Village Community, 44
Village Panchayats, 44
Voluntary Organizations (VOs), 52, 88, 136, 167, 237-254

W

Western Industrialized Nations, 40
Westernization, 163, 218
Widow Remarriage, 231
Widowed Elderly, 137
Widowhood, 227, 229, 232, 233, 235
Women Farmers' Interest Group, 37
World Assembly on Ageing, 159, 167, 174, 209, 251
World Health Organization (WHO), 25, 31, 51, 64, 98

Y

Yoga, 54
Yoga Exercises, 84